AT PLAYSCHOOL WITH MARY MY MOTHER

Jack McArdle ss cc

At Playschool with Mary my Mother

SIMPLE TEACHINGS ON THE BASICS

the columba press

First published in 2006 by
the columba press
55A Spruce Avenue, Stillorgan Industrial Park,
Blackrock, Co Dublin

Cover by Bill Bolger
Cover photograph shows Fr Jack preparing to carry the statue
in procession at Lourdes
Origination by The Columba Press
Printed in Ireland by ColourBooks Ltd, Dublin

ISBN 1 85607 520 6

Table of Contents

Introduction

This book is something that has been with me for a long time now. I constantly find a need to return to the basics. As someone who spent many years as a teacher, I appreciate the treasure of having a good teacher. A good teacher, in my definition, is someone who is 'present' to the pupil, and not someone who is speaking from some lofty height of abstract knowledge. The teacher must have a particular interest in the subject being taught, and an even greater interest in the pupils being taught. Someone who loves and respects his subject, and his pupils, is probably a good teacher. When I decided to return to basics, I could think of no greater teacher than Mary my Mother. After all, she was there from the very beginning, and she has had a central role to play in the story of our salvation since. As far as it was possible for me, I let her lead, allowed her do the talking, and some of the titles of the chapters took me by surprise! I tried to make the situation as real as I could, and I tried not to let my attention wander from myself at my Mother's knee. I'm sorry, gentle reader, but, as I wrote, I didn't have you in mind at all!

Now that the book is ready to be prepared for publication, and to end up in your hands, I have to share with you the enormous joy I experienced in the writing. I genuinely found the experience both warm and personal. I was very conscious of the privilege that was mine, and I genuinely tried to be scrupulously faithful to what I believed she would say about any particular subject. This is difficult to achieve, because there is always the danger that my own ideas and opinions might get in the way. I know, of course, that she could also use those, but I would like to think that I did succeed in keeping out of the way as much as possible.

In the course of each session, I interrupt with about three questions. The questions are ones that I really did want/need to ask. There were other questions, but I did not think them important enough to break the flow of what was being presented. Asking the questions also gave me a chance to tune in further to the subject under discussion, and the times spent away from the computer were times of reflection and learning insights. Writing this book has been my 'prayer-life' for the past two weeks. It was a wonderful and happy experience, and something for which I am truly grateful. Over the past few years I have exchanged 'devotion to Mary' with 'a relationship with Mary'. I can honestly say that she is *now* my Mother. This has been a gradual process, but a very worthwhile one. The writing of this book was inevitable, because I found myself speaking more and more to others about attending her Playschool. I began this approach almost a year ago, when I took a few days out for prayer and reflection. It just *happened*, that's all I can say. From the very beginning, I knew that this is what I really wanted to do, and I have been returning to that Playschool on many occasions since. A slow learner?

I let go of this book now with a certain sadness. This surprises me, because I know that my Mother is still with me, and she will continue to teach me. Maybe because I spent many hours each day, over a two-week period, very conscious of her presence, I have a feeling that my office might feel empty now. I know, however, that she would want me to share this with others, because it is not my personal possession. Having had the privilege of writing is something that I appreciate. I pray for you, gentle reader, that you too will experience her loving presence as you read.

CHAPTER ONE

God

One of the first points that you have to grasp is that what I tell you is too much for you to understand. I can use words that you understand, and concepts and ideas that are familiar to you in everyday living, yet the *truth* behind what I say can be completely hidden from you. You are limited('boxed-in') in your human nature. You can see and hear those things that are within your reach. There are people speaking to each other a few miles from where you are now, but you cannot see them, or hear them without the help of something electronic, such as a telephone, or a television. What I will speak to you about is even beyond the scope of anything electronic. I will obtain for you the gift of understanding things beyond your human understanding, and of seeing things, and understanding truths that are away beyond your human vision, or your mental capacity. Imagine two boxes on the floor in front of you. One is quite small, while the other is so huge that you cannot possibly see around it, or over it. I will take truths from that large box, and present them to you in such a simple way that all of the truths in that large box will fit into the little box, which represents you. Don't worry how I will do that! That's my responsibility and, as I work with you, you will understand more and more the wonderful mysteries and secrets of God. In many and varied ways I will teach you, and lead you into a deep conviction about the truths I share with you.

Let's look at that word *God* for a moment. The concept of God is so far beyond your mind to grasp that, when you speak about him, you are certain to be wrong! He is so much more than anything you could say about him. And yet that same God, almighty and infinite, can give you a special vision to see him, and an extraordinary mind to know him. It's like as if God could pour all the oceans on earth into a small teacup. I hope you are beginning to get excited about this, because it is truly wonderful and absolutely mind-boggling. The first thing I want you to know is that there is only *one* God; God with a capital G. There are many other gods (small g) which people worship, such as money, power, or pleasure. The world is full of such false gods. That is why I must make it clear, right at the beginning, that there is only *one true* God. Right from the beginning, I will give you another word for the God of which I speak, and that word is *love*. Always be ready to switch from one word to the other, and know that you are speaking about the same thing. You probably smiled when I used the word 'love', because you know what that means. The truth is, of course, that you know very little about love, but you have a few ideas about it. What you know already will be a good starting place, and I will build on that to complete the picture. Yes, indeed, *God is love*, and everything *he* says and does is done out of love. For example, he decided that you should exist, so he created you, and that was a beautiful act of love.

I'll give you a break for a moment, because you might have some questions you want to ask.

I have many questions, but the one I would love you to answer is: You said that God created me as an expression of his love. What about the millions of other children he creates that have very short and painful lives, because of the lack of food or medicine, or the presence of war or natural disasters? Surely he's not doing them any great favour by creating them?

Wow, that's a good question! I will answer it in part now, because we will be coming back to this on several other occasions, in connection with other questions. Love must be something that is *freely* given, otherwise, it is not real love. If I *have* to love you, and have no choice, then that's not real love at all. When God created you he left you with a choice, a decision. He gave you a gift that would make it possible for you to love others the way he loves us. In other words, he made you in his image and likeness. However, he didn't create you in such a way that you *have* to love others, and have no choice in the matter. He gave us what we call 'free will'. We are *free* to love, or not to love; that choice is ours. It is obvious which choice God wants us to make, but he won't interfere, if we choose not to love. If we loved the way God loves us, then there would be no hunger, no wars, or no environmental damage, which causes most of our natural disasters. There is enough food for everyone, but those who have plenty refuse to share with those who have nothing. Each of us is part of a team. If you refuse to pass on the baton, then you will lose the relay race. Some people believe that if God would change, and do things differently, everything would be ok; while God *knows* that if we changed, and did things differently, yes, indeed, all would be well. God never planted a bomb, fired a bullet, or took food out of the mouths of the hungry. It is not God's will that people should kill each other, or that people die of hunger because others won't let them have food. I'm sure you are aware of the wonderful efforts of good people to correct these wrongs. These people are an example to all others, and if each person followed their example, the world would be completely changed for the better. That is what God asks of us, but he does not *demand* anything, because he has given us free will, and our response must be voluntary; it must be something that we ourselves decide to do. To watch my children crying and dying breaks my heart, and that's exactly why I'm speaking to you now. I believe that *you* can make a difference. There was never a bullet fired or a bomb planted that did not begin in the heart of some individual. It is the same with the process of goodness. You can be like a stone thrown into a pond, which sends rings out to the very edge.

I said that we would return to your questions many times during our time together. For now, however, all I ask for is that *you* decide for the good … and much good will follow for many others.

Before your question, I was speaking about God being love.

This means that God loves us 100%, and could not possibly love us less. His love is constant, and there are no conditions. For example, God doesn't tell us that, if we're good, he'll love us. No, he loves us because he is good, no matter what we're like. Suppose you are in your bedroom, with the light on. The room is bright, and you can see clearly. You decide to leave your room, and go out into a dark corridor. You are now in the dark, and you can see nothing. Remember, however, that the light is still shining in the room, even when you decided to walk away from it. God's love is still there, even if we choose to live outside or apart from it. I am praying for you as I speak to you, because, of yourself, you could never grasp these truths. Even if you knew that God loved you, it might be nothing more than knowledge up in your head. I want you to know this *down in your heart*. In other words, it's the most important thing that you could possibly know and believe. Knowing that God loves you is much more important than you loving God. A good definition of a saint is not somebody who loves God, but someone who is convinced that God loves her. I have so many things to teach you, but it is essential that you get this simple truth embedded in your heart first. When I speak to you about *what* God is doing for you, or wants to do for you, it will be so much easier to grasp if you have a deep conviction about *why* he loves you. He has made you in such a way that you are an extension of him, and he never ever wants to be separated from you. He looks upon you, and he sees you as no other human being ever could. He sees a reflection of himself when he looks at you. When he sees brokenness and sin he only wants to remove it, because it doesn't belong there. He sees you as being worth much more than you yourself could possibly imagine.

God never remains still; he is always active. Oh, yes, he created you, but he *continues* to create you with each new day. (He loves you as you are, but he loves you more than that, or otherwise he would leave you as you are !) You are clay in the hands of God, the Master Potter. He is continually shaping you, and forming you until you are a perfect reflection of what he had in mind when he called you into existence. Don't forget what I told you about free will. It sounds crazy but, in your case, the clay can actually resist the hands of the Potter, and decide for itself how it wants to be formed. The results can be truly beautiful, or very very ugly. The choice is yours. Please remember what I told you earlier, and don't even try to understand this. All I ask is that you trust me, and believe me now, and all the rest will follow. As I speak to you, I am praying for you, asking God to give you the *gift* of opening your heart to the truths I present to you. Don't worry about the *understanding* … that will come later.

There is so much I want to tell you, but I want to stay with the theme of God, love, and you, until I feel you have absorbed the truth behind it, and you *know* what I know. It will change your life totally. Just leave to one side, for a while, all your faults and failings, and join with me in standing before God as you would before the midday sun. Let the warmth of his love touch your spirit, and melt away all the crusts of fear, loneliness, guilt, and isolation that you wrap yourself in. Let the warmth of his love seep into the very core of your being, and melt any coldness that may have gathered around your heart. Imagine you are sitting out in the back garden on a deck-chair on a sunny summer's day. All you have to do is *be* there; the sun will do the rest. Don't worry about sun-burn; I will protect you with my mantle. When you leave aside the faults and failings (for a while), what's left is what God created. When exposed to the warmth of his love, it is so much easier for the Potter to melt and to mould. One of the great mistakes that people make is to believe that they must make themselves perfect before they have any right to stand before God. Oh, what a great mistake that is! If you wait till that time, then the first time you are going to stand before God is at the moment of death. It could be too late then! The problem here is a very simple one; it is a question of where and how to start. You begin *exactly as you are*, and *then* the changes begin to happen. This is something that you *experience* firstly, and come to *understand* later on.

How are we doing so far? Any questions?

Yes, I was wondering does all of this happen suddenly, or does it take time? If it takes time, how much time are we talking about?

Once again, a good question. The handiest way to answer is to say that it happens suddenly, but it will take you time to become aware of the change. You have spent quite a while with certain beliefs and attitudes, and it will take some time to let go of these, and then to realise that they are gone. Take the example of your mother steeping some whites in bleach. Once she has submerged the articles in the liquid, the process has already begun. (By the way, that word 'process' is a very useful word in helping you grasp some of what I'm saying.) It means a series of ongoing changes; things that happen as time goes on. That is how you will change. The process begins immediately and, as time goes on, you will become more aware of what's happening. If you have a younger brother or sister, you may have noticed how the hair grew, and the teeth appeared, and the baby did nothing to cause any of this! This is actually God continuing to create the baby. I can see by that expression on your face that you have another question!

Yes, I have. If God is continuing to create the baby, why would he let the baby get leukaemia, meningitis, or be found dead in its cot?

Yes, that's a *big* one, and I'll help you understand something about that. I'm delighted you asked it, because it shows that I have your attention. *What God creates is good.* His grace, however, builds on nature, and does not replace it. What I mean by that is that God creates the *person*, while the *body* is a combination of the genes, personality traits, and 'humanness' of the parents. That means that the baby's body contains within itself all that is good and bad within the parents. If the parents are tall and slim, it is likely that the baby will grow to become tall and slim. If the parents are of a nervous disposition, and subject to depression and paranoia, it is likely that the baby will grow up with many emotional problems. The human body is made up of a certain and particular chemistry. One body is very much effected by hay fever, while another never has a breathing problem of any kind. One body reacts to the toxins in the air, and develops cancerous growths, while another seems to be completely immune to all such influences. This is *nature* taking its course, and God allows nature to follow its course. Grace (God's blessing) builds on nature; it doesn't replace it. Nature has an extraordinary way of accommodating to its conditions. The blind can have very sharp hearing, or a very sharp sense of touch. One of Ireland's greatest artists was born without arms, and painted and wrote with his feet. People in different parts of the world have skins that are black, white, brown, or yellow. The chemistry of some bodies cause them to grow to an abnormal height, while others remain away below the height of the normal. Some have eyes that cannot see, or ears that cannot hear. All of this has to do with the *body*. The *person* inside is fully human and fully alive, even if the mind is not fully functional. The most disabled child is on this earth with as much right as the greatest genius that ever lived. What the body can do, or what the body or mind can achieve, is not a test of the value of the person. It is the *person* living within the body that matters.

I'm sorry if all of this seems 'heavy' and difficult to grasp. However, I know that we will come back to all of this in several more of our sessions together. I am very conscious of the fact that many such questions make no sense whatever to the human mind, and I trust the Spirit of God to enlighten you about all such questions. Speaking of the Spirit of God reminds me that it's time we moved on, and our next session together will deal with the whole question of the Trinity, the Father, Son, and Holy Spirit.

Before we finish off today, I want to summarise what I have been telling you. I want you to *know* God and his *love*. I want you to be open to that love, so that you can grow in the warmth of that love. I want you to live a life that is blessed with God's love and care, so that you can pass this message on to others as you travel along the road of life. I am speaking to you personally, but I am very conscious of all the others who can be touched for good by you, and by your example. You are very precious to me, and I have chosen you because you have the disposition to listen to me, and to learn from me. This gives me great happiness, and I rejoice in the knowledge of how much happiness all of this will bring to you. I will pray for you very especially. Thank you for listening. I'll see you tomorrow.

CHAPTER TWO

Father, Son and Spirit

Welcome back. Today's lesson will require your full attention, although, of course, you will get the grace to know what I am saying. The Blessed Trinity is a mystery, that is, it is beyond the human mind to understand. I am not going to *explain* the Trinity to you, but I will give you insights that will enable you accept it, and take it on board as something which you believe. I said in our last chat that there is only *one* God. That is still true. God, of course, can *express* himself in as many ways as he chooses. He appeared to Moses as a burning bush, and he spoke to the prophet in a gentle breeze. Because God is the source of life, it is right to call him Father. In the Old Testament (with the Jews), he was their God, and they were his people. In the New Testament (with the Christians), he is the Father, and they are his children. You may have been blessed with a good father as you were growing up; therefore the word 'Father' means something good to you. Others may not have been so blessed, and the word 'Father' may not have any connection with love. That is why it is vitally important to grasp this concept of Father right from the start, no matter what your own personal experience has been. You can begin right *now*, just as if you never heard the word 'Father' before. The father is a provider, a protector, who looks out at all times for the good and welfare of his family. (Don't worry, I will deal with Mother is a separate session!) God is the Father who creates life, and who provides all that is needed to live that life. Later on, when we speak about you being a child, this concept of Father will mean much more to you. For now, however, let us plod along.

Love is something that is impossible to understand. It is continually active, creating, doing new things, and is always giving. God is love, and so the same can be said of him. God *had* to create the world, with you and me in it, because love needs to *share*. If love is not shared, it is no longer love. When people chose to reject God's love, God did not change his mind about loving. He humoured the spoilt children that we are, and he came up with another way of loving us. There is no way that he could let go of us. He created us as part of himself, and he would never want us to be separated from him. He reached out a hand to us, and that hand is the person we call Jesus. Jesus is not different from the Father, nor is he a different God. 'They who hear me, hear the Father; and they who see me see the Father', he told us. If we were unwilling to share in God's Divinity, then God would come and share in our humanity. When God created people 'He saw that they were good.' Adam and Eve believed the lies of Satan, and so human nature became corrupted. There was darkness now where there used to be light. When God decided to save us he was going to reach out one arm and remove the viruses that corrupted human nature. This arm of God is the one we call Jesus, because Jesus means 'Saviour'. Jesus would be entrusted with half the work. He would repair the damage of original sin, and then the other arm of God (the Holy Spirit) would come to apply the results of Jesus' life and death to our lives, so that the two arms could gather us into the eternal hug of the Father. All of this is God expressing himself in different ways. Look at it this way. I place three things in front of you, an ice cube, a snowball, and a glass of water. It wouldn't take you long to discern that, despite the appearance, all I have given you is water. Whether we think of God, or look upon him as Father, Jesus, or Holy Spirit, we are still speaking of the same God.

By the way, how are we doing? Any questions coming up?

I know what you're saying, ok, but I'm puzzled that God would go to so much trouble to humour us, when he could have scrapped the whole idea, or come up with a plan that would make us earn our own salvation. Why would God bother?

The part of your question that is easiest to deal with is the idea of you earning your own salvation. That is *out … out … out*. There is *no way* you could make your way back to God (the Garden) on your own. Be very definite about that one. Therefore, whatever hope you have, it just has to be *pure free gift* … something you could never earn or merit. The big words we use for this are redemption, or salvation. In this way we are offered a passport, a visa, and a green card for heaven. The extraordinary thing is that many people still choose to say No! They either don't want the gift, or they insist on doing things their way, and doing everything for themselves. Again, here's where the extraordinary nature of love comes in. Love allows them to be or to do whatever they choose, and will always be there to welcome them back, if and when they realise the error of their ways. If they choose not to come back to love, then they have put themselves outside of that love for all eternity. Even at that last moment, love has to allow *freedom*, and will never *compel* a response that is not given with the free will of the person. God just could not scrap the whole idea, because God's love cannot cease; it must continue to flow, and to create, whether we respond or not. God arranged things so, and he cannot go against his own plans.

Jesus took on the viruses of our corruption – sin, sickness, and death – and he had to overcome each one in turn. The Jews offered a lamb to God for the forgiveness of their sins. They killed the lamb (the innocent one), and burned it, so that the smoke would ascend towards heaven, as a prayer. Jesus called himself the Lamb of God because, as the innocent one, he was going to take on the sins of the world. Like a surgeon removing a cancerous growth, he would remove the evil of sin from us. Even after surgery, the patient will still be on treatment, to ensure that the cancer does not return. For the sinner there is a treatment called repentance, which is an on-going acknowledgement of our sins, and a willingness to accept the forgiveness and redemption of Jesus. From the time you accept this redemption of Jesus – I mean as an adult who is aware of what it means – you are continually in treatment for your condition until you arrive into the perfection and fullness of heaven. Another way of putting this is that you accept the fact that you are a sinner, but you also *know* that you have a Saviour, and all is well. It's like having a problem, and a solution to the problem at the one time. Only God is perfect. As long as you are human, you will have weaknesses and problems, but I want to tell you something about that that should make all the difference in the world. God's power works best in human weakness. If you didn't have the weakness, you would never have an opportunity to experience God's power. This is something that we will deal with at greater length in a later session.

I said that Jesus came to take away the sins of the world. He also came to take away sickness. This requires some explanation. Sickness is not a good thing. It must never be confused with *suffering*. Suffering is a gift from God for very special souls, who are asked to join with Jesus in making reparation for the sins of the world. Such souls give extraordinary witness, such as Francis of Assisi or Padre Pio. Sickness is something else altogether. It implies a dis-ease, a lack of well-being, a system that has broken down. It is difficult to find anything good in it, unless the person concerned has the necessary faith to turn even sickness into a good. If you are sick, you can turn to God for help. When God answers your prayers he will either remove the sickness, or he will turn your sickness into suffering, and you will have the grace to grow and to have peace with your condition. This can be as great a miracle as if God removed the sickness completely.

The third virus that Jesus overcomes is death. Nobody wants to die, and death runs completely contrary to our instinct for self-preservation. Through his death and resurrection, Jesus took the sting out of death, and he has turned it into a *birth*, through which we pass on into eternal life. Death is no longer the *end* but the *beginning* of something new. It becomes a *victory* that frees you from all the weaknesses and limitations of your human nature. That is why people of faith can look forward to death, when they can become all that God created them to be.

From the moment of birth until death you are imprisoned in the body, and are unable to live life to the full. Death releases you from prison, and allows you the freedom to *fly*. Have you ever imagined what it must be like to be able to fly, to rise away above everything here on earth, and to see beyond horizons, and to understand beyond reason? Jesus has turned death into a *triumph* when, as the song says, 'the saints go marching in'. You very well may have a question or two about all of this, so feel free to ask.

Surely Jesus could have done all that he did without having to come on this earth as a helpless infant, live his life amidst great struggles, and suffer an ignominious and shameful death?

Indeed he could; of course he could. However, he understands human beings so well that he needed to identify totally with them. By joining in the human journey we can never doubt that he completely understands our struggles and our strives. He became like you in all things, so that he could experience hunger, loneliness, rejection, pain, suffering and death. He wants to walk the walk with you. He wants to accompany you, and to lead you, as Moses led the Hebrews, until you arrive safely in the promised land. He needed a hand to hold yours, and a voice to teach you his message. He needed to *do* everything he would ask you to do. He acted first, and then he taught. He washed feet, and told his apostles how they should treat one another. If he did not have a body he would only be a ghost, and his words and actions would have no relevance to the lives of those who followed him. In human terms, for Jesus to become *real* (credible?) He had to take on our human nature, and become just as we are.

The third way in which God expresses himself is as the Holy Spirit. When Jesus had completed his mission, he returned to the glory of the Father. He then sent the Holy Spirit to complete his work on earth. The Holy Spirit is like the breath and power of God. When God created people, he formed a figure out of clay (the Potter) and of course this would be no more than a statue. He then breathed his Spirit into the clay, and he created the first person. He gave life to the clay. When he created the world, his Spirit hovered over the chaos, and brought order out of chaos, so we had land, sea, and sky. God's Spirit was involved at all points of new birth in this world. When the Archangel Gabriel asked me to agree to a plan that God had devised to save the world, I was, naturally, afraid, and could never agree to accept such an impossibility. But when I was told that the Spirit of God would come upon me, I had no problem in agreeing, because God was going to supply the power, was going to make it possible. For the first thirty years of his life Jesus was just like everybody else, except, of course, there was always something special about him. Then, one day, as he stood in the waters of the river Jordan, the Spirit came upon him, and his mission was launched. No matter what Jesus told his disciples, or what they saw him doing, they were totally unprepared to take on any mission. At Pentecost, however, the Spirit came upon them, and they came out of that room completely changed, and ready to go to the ends of the earth to proclaim his message, and to pay for that with their lives.

There are two parts to the story of salvation. There is what Jesus did, and how you respond to that. What you must remember, however, is that even the response part is done by God, and is the unique work of the Holy Spirit. If you do not have the Holy Spirit within your heart, you will be unable to respond to all that Jesus earned for you, and you will not be able to return to the Father. Jesus and the Holy Spirit are like two arms of God that stretch out to embrace you, and draw you to himself. Supposing you drew a large triangle on a piece of paper. There are three points on the triangle. The top point represents the Father, the one on the bottom left represents Jesus, and the one on the bottom right represents the Holy Spirit. That is why the Holy Trinity is often represented by a Triangle. You remain outside of that triangle *until you decide that you want to belong in the middle.* You hear the Father's invitation to come back to him with all your heart. You hear Jesus telling you that no one can come to the Father except through him. You hear the Holy Spirit telling you not to fear, because he will give you what it takes to avail of the whole gift of salvation. Ah, I can see that you have a question! Right?

Yes, you're right. I know there's only one God, *but how do I distinguish between the Father, Son, and Spirit, if I want to come to God, if I want to pray to him? If I pray to the Father, am I praying to the Son and the Spirit at the same time? Does it matter which of them I pray to, or is each of them a 'specialist' in some particular area of life?*

A lovely question, and it makes me smile! There is only one God (I repeat), but God expresses himself in three different ways. To help us form a concept of this we refer to each expression as a Person. There are three Persons in the one God. Let us take somebody called George, for example. He is a general in the army. He then is appointed an ambassador for his country in some other country. At a subsequent election, he is elected President of his country. We are still talking about George here, even though his roles change dramatically. I know he is still George. It would be unrealistic to think of him as President as being exactly as he was when he was a soldier in the army. God can go one beyond poor George! In each role, he can be a separate Person, while still being part of the One God. We represent the Father as a father-figure; Jesus as being a Jew of many years ago; and the Spirit as being a Dove … as the wind beneath our wings, that enables us fly. It matters nothing which expression of God you speak to. Sometimes when you are lonely, you need the presence of a Father. When you feel broken and a failure, you turn to Jesus for forgiveness and healing. When you need guidance and direction in making a decision, you turn to the Holy Spirit. It is just wonderful how God accommodates himself to meet us as we are. Some people are totally at ease being part of the Trinity, and they make no distinction of Persons. Others are very conscious of their dependence on the guidance and

power of the Spirit. Others, yet again, because of their brokenness and failures, can relate more easily with Jesus the Saviour
who forgives and heals. And then there are those who, because
of having the heart of a child, can feel totally comfortable with a
God who is a Father. Please be at ease with what your heart tells
you, knowing that when you pray to one, you are praying to all.

I want to repeat something that I will continue to repeat. We
are dealing with mystery here, so you cannot expect to *understand* it. That is not what I'm trying to do, nor is it what I wish. I
will pray for you, and I will ask the Holy Spirit to enlighten you,
so that your spirit can become as open as is possible to the fullness of God. Remember it is only God who can pour all the
oceans into a small teacup. All I ask is that you accept what I
share with you, and be certain that, as time goes on, it will continue to become more and more real to you. I was tempted to say
'it will mean more to you', but that would be a mistake. You will
never grasp or understand it in your head, but you will know it
in your heart.

Let me give you a little example that might help you.
Supposing John has a lovely new car, and it is stolen. Imagine
his upset. A day or two later, however, the car is recovered, and
the person who stole it is arrested. John goes down to the police
station, and he comes face to face with the person who stole his
car. We won't pretend to guess what he might do or say! Would
you think John is crazy if he forgave the person, gave him a present of the car, and gave him a credit card that would entitle him
to free petrol for the rest of his life? What's a bigger word than
'crazy'? I use this as a way of showing how God treated us.
Human beings decided that they would become like God.
Instead of punishing them, God decided on a plan (salvation)
that would enable them share in his Divinity, and he supplied
the power (Holy Spirit) that would enable them live as part of
his Divinity for all eternity. That is what the Trinity makes possible. We refer to the Trinity as Father, Son and Holy Spirit, and I
believe it can help us to keep that order, when we think of the
different roles that each plays in our salvation. We begin our

prayers, and bless ourselves, using these three titles. The ideal is to be absorbed into the life of the Trinity, and to have a sense of *belonging* to God in every way. Despite all the wonderful things that happened to me, all of this never ceases to astound me. The more I *magnify* God, the bigger he becomes. Some people have a God that is far too small. That is why their problems appear to be so huge. The bigger your God, the smaller your problems. 'Nothing is impossible with God' is something I was told right at the very beginning, and I still marvel at just how very true that is. It is my great desire to pray for you, so that you get some concept of an almighty and infinite God, whose main concern is all that is best for you. God is infinite and he can afford to see each person as a single individual, and not just one in a crowd. *You* do matter to him. If you were the only person on this planet, all that Jesus did, and the Spirit does, would surely happen anyhow; because, without that, you would be eternally lost. I spoke of the Trinity as being three Persons. You can become a *fourth* person, and your life can become inseparable from the life of the Trinity. I would like to believe, even from the very fact that you are listening to me now, that you have what it takes to avail of this extraordinary privilege. That is my prayer for you; that is my hope for you; that is my goal for you. May the Trinity bless you, and thank you for listening.

CHAPTER THREE

Myself!

Let me be very clear about one thing right from the start here. If I speak about *myself* it is only because I want to share with you what God has done for and with me. You see, if you know what he has done for me, you can have a much better idea of what he wants to do for you. I'm not sure that people realise the fact that God actually *chooses* each of us to perform a particular task. For example, there are things for which you are chosen, and if you don't do them, they will never be done. You saw an old lady struggling with a heavy load today, and you kept going, and didn't stop to help. The woman did not get help, because you were the only one around. 'I shall pass this way but once. Any good deed that I can do, any good word that I can say, let me do it now, let me say it now, for I shall never pass this way again.' During this day alone you have had many opportunities to say the kind word or to do the kind deed. Did you avail of the opportunities? Did you even realise that God may have chosen you to say that word, or do that deed? God has no other hands or feet or voice but ours. God endowed me with a very precious gift, and I have to sincerely and gratefully acknowledge that. He let me see both sides of the one coin at the same time. I saw clearly that, of myself, I could do nothing but, with God, I could do anything. Without this second part of the gift, I would have eked out a life in some mud-cabin, slaving to meet my obligations, and totally bereft of any joy, or sense of purpose. If you were to ask me why God chose to give me this special gift, all I can answer is that he chose me, because he could have chosen *anyone* he wanted. Does that make any sense to you? He had to choose someone, and that someone happened to be me. I had nothing to do with the decision to choose. I was unaware that I had this special gift, because I thought that everyone else had it too. My parents were very special people, and I wouldn't dare think I might have a gift that they didn't have.

The ways of God are mysterious, and it is not for us to understand or question them. I had no idea that God had a very special plan for me and I'm glad I didn't, because the thought of it would have frightened me. As I grew older I became more and more aware of the power, the wisdom, and the glory of God. Compared to this, my vision of myself could only fade towards nothingness. As God seemed to grow so much bigger, so I myself seemed to grow so much smaller. This brought me to a point where I saw myself as being nothing, and of having nothing apart from God. My soul just worshipped in quiet awe, and I never ceased to be amazed as I stood before his infinite glory. My soul hungered and thirsted for his light and his life. Everything in this world seemed like litter that is blown in the wind. I had no interest in chasing that litter, because my heart was flooded with light and a gentle peace. Even if the Archangel Gabriel never appeared to me, I still knew that I was special, and that God was spoiling me completely. I tried to mind my own business, so I wasn't sure how other people felt, but I assumed that many of them were having an experience similar to mine.

Like all other Jews of that time, I longed and prayed for the promised Messiah. On many occasions God had brought back my people out of exile and slavery. This time we were not in Egypt or Babylon, but we were slaves within our own country. The idea of a Messiah had more to do with ridding us of the control of the Romans than bringing us closer to God. I had no idea what God had in mind, but I felt that if God was going to do something it would have to do with bringing us closer to him. I was taken completely by surprise when the Archangel told me that I was chosen to be part of God's plan. I didn't know what that plan was but, once I was assured that this is something that *God* would do, I had no problem in agreeing to it. Who was I to question or oppose what God wanted to do? My first reaction was to be afraid, which is quite understandable when an Archangel stands in front of you! I asked just one question – how can I do this? – and when I was told that the Holy Spirit would do all that was needed, I had no hesitation in saying my *Yes*. I had no idea then that my *Yes* was to reverse the effects of the *No* of Adam and Eve. I was caught in a bind, because I was engaged to Joseph, and was to be married to him shortly. How was I going to explain to him (and to the world) that I was already pregnant, and was going to give birth to a baby as a result of a direct intervention of God? My problem was solved when an angel appeared to Joseph in a dream, and set his mind at rest about the whole thing. I had no clear idea what exactly was going on, but I never questioned God's plan for me, and I trusted that all would be well. I would never dream of questioning God's wisdom. All I knew was that it was my role to obey, and to trust. I *know* that you have a question. Go ahead …

Your trust in God frightens me! You ran the great risk of becoming an unmarried mother, of being exposed as an immoral person, and risked being stoned to death. Did you ever think of that?

No, to tell you the truth, I didn't. I can't explain this, but there was something within me that gave me complete confidence that all of this was from God, and that he could be relied on to see it through. Even if I were to end up being stoned to death, I was sure that I had no other choice than to obey his wishes for me. In time, of course, I became more and more convinced that the Holy Spirit was in charge, and all that was happening was completely beyond my control. It was as if the Holy Spirit filled the sails of my little boat, and I allowed myself to drift out into deep and uncharted waters. I just went with the flow and, like the seagull, I felt that I was riding the wind. I learned to live with mystery, and to allow a Higher Power take over. I knew that I myself was away out of my depth, and I had no choice but to let go, and let God. It might help you to understand that I don't think of myself *doing* anything; but I allowed God do what he wanted with me. That's what always amazed me, and still fills my soul with joy, and gladness. At the time, my trust in God was much stronger than my fears for myself. Naturally, I thought a lot about it, because I didn't fully understand what was going on, but I never wavered in my conviction that God was in charge.

For most of my life with Jesus I was always conscious of living in faith. Joseph was just wonderful, and I depended a lot on him. My visit to Elizabeth was a very special occasion. I was caught in a bind, and I saw no way around it. What had happened to me (Archangel Gabriel) was so strange that I couldn't speak to anybody about it. I might not have been stoned to death, but I would be the butt of ridicule and derision. I *needed* to talk to somebody who would understand. I said that Joseph was wonderful, but I needed to share with another woman, and with a woman who would understand. Elizabeth was always special to me as I grew up, and I felt certain that she, of all people, would be a safe confidant. Imagine my amazement and joy when she spoke first, and I *knew* that she knew! That was an extraordinary experience. A song of joy and praise welled up in my heart, and I just sang the feelings that were within. 'My soul magnifies the Lord, and my spirit rejoices in God my Saviour; because he that is mighty has done great things for me, and holy is his name ...' We hugged and we cried together. She too had good reason to rejoice, and I was so happy for her. I look back now and I like to think that my visit to Elizabeth was a beautiful preparation for Bethlehem, when Joseph and myself would be on our own again. It may seem strange to you but Bethlehem was very ordinary. No fireworks or sound of angels' wings! I was totally at *peace*, and nothing seemed to worry me. As I held that child, my heart was pounding with love, my soul was filled with peace and joy, and my mind was totally blank! I just couldn't take in what all of this meant. Later, when the shepherds and Wise Men came, I realised that this event had not just happened to me, but to the *world*. I kept concentrating on each passing moment, and I left the future entirely in God's hands. I was given another little glimpse of the infinite possibilities that surrounded me, when we went to the Temple, and met Simeon, a very old man of God. I always held such people in high reverence any time I visited the Temple when I was growing up. Imagine my delight when he took the child in his arms, and spoke his words of prophecy. He was now happy to die, because he had encountered this very special child. (He didn't use the word 'God', nor did I think the word 'God'. At that time I just knew he was *special*.) Some of what Simeon said caused me to reflect. He spoke about this child being sent for 'the resurrection and the fall of many in Israel'. I wasn't sure what he meant by that, but I took it that some would accept him, and others would reject him. He spoke about a sword piercing my own heart, and that stirred some anxiety within me, until I regained my normal composure, and remembered that it was all in God's hands.

The marriage in Cana marked a breakthrough for all of us. I was at the Jordan when Jesus went down into the waters. I saw the Spirit come upon him, and I heard the Father's voice saying 'This is My Beloved Son, in whom I am well pleased.' I didn't speak to Jesus about this, but I had a much more heightened awareness when I was in his presence. The young couple in Cana who got married were friends of mine. It was I who got the invitation, but I was told to bring Jesus as well. I knew that none of them had noticed or heard anything wonderful about him, so it would be safe to bring him along. I was helping out at the serving and, as it happened, I was the first to notice that the wine was nearly all gone. Everybody was having such a happy time, and the young couple were so delighted that it broke my heart to have to tell them the bad news. This would have been a mark of disgrace and ridicule in those days. I felt that I had no choice, so I took a deep breath, went straight to Jesus, and told him about the problem. He was taken by surprise, as if I had sprung something on him before he was prepared. However, I just looked at him, and he looked at me, and then I *knew*! This was it! I just told the servants what to do, and I slipped back into the kitchen. My heart was doing somersaults. To me he was

Jesus, but I was also *certain* that God was in our midst. His mission had begun. Later, I would be with him when his work was completed, and that was a much less joyous occasion. I will come to that shortly. I'll give you a break for a while, in case you have a question for me. Ok?

Yes, I have. You amaze me how you always seem to have lived on the edge, not afraid to take risks, and never hesitating about stepping out. Can you understand now just what prompted you to walk up to Jesus and ask for a miracle? That could turn out to be extraordinary faith, or extreme foolishness.

Yes, I still smile when I think of that moment. With hindsight, of course, it was the right and the only thing to do. I see now that it was the Holy Spirit inviting Jesus to step out, and to begin his mission. I was just being used to bring this about. I had a sense of certainty and expectation that just *had* to be a gift from God. I didn't *think* about it at all, and I'm glad I didn't. Sometimes when you think about something, the head takes over, all the fears come to the surface, and you do nothing. Fear can make cowards of us all. I had always known, from the time he was a child, that love just oozed out of Jesus. I was certain that he *would* help if he could, and I had a real strong feeling that he could. I never ever thought of Jesus as someone who would let me down, or refuse to do as I requested. (By the way, that is just as true *today*.) How I wish that *you* might, at least sometimes, have the feeling that I had at Cana, and then you too would have your own miracles.

For the next three years Jesus' life was hectic. So many people flocked around him, so many came to him as their last hope in desperation, that I just wanted to keep out of the way, and not take up any of his time. He always made a point of being in touch, of course, but he also knew that I was happy to stay in the background, watching, listening and praying. I found out more about him by watching what he did, and listening to what he said, than in speaking directly with him. (I recommend that to you as you read the gospels. Just concentrate on what he says and does, and you will come to know him on a very personal level.) I had a small group of friends who kept close to me, and we were there for each other. All of us saw the clouds gathering towards the end. It was obvious that the religious leaders could not permit him to expose them, oppose them, and condemn them as he did. I was very attentive whenever he spoke about his coming suffering and death. I was sure that he meant it, and I was sure that it would happen. This was the most difficult part of my whole life. Of course, I still trusted that all was safe in God's hands, but I dared to hope that suffering and death would not be part of the package. Eventually, I just *knew*, and from that moment, I prepared myself for the inevitable. Oh how I loved him, and how I would willingly take his place for that final part of his mission. It was a very lonely time, because even my closest friends could never possibly accept that his mission could be stopped, and he could be killed. They were convinced that his power would bring him safely through each and every danger. There were a few close calls, when his enemies tried to arrest him, stone him, or throw him over a cliff, and each time he just walked away, and they stood there powerless. My friends were convinced that this is how it would continue to be. However, I *knew*, I just knew.

No matter what was going to happen, my mission was quite clear. My mission was to be *there* for him, through thick and through thin. Whether he lived, or whether he died, I would be there for him, and with him. When the time came, the apostles were amazed at what they called my bravery. They didn't understand. Jesus and myself had become so bound to each other that I could not possibly be separated from him. As I stood by his cross on the Hill of Calvary, there was just one thing that kept me going. *I knew this was not the end.* I had heard him predict his suffering and death, but I had also heard him predict his resurrection, and I believed and accepted *all* that he said. For his disciples, Calvary was a disaster, where all their hopes and dreams were shattered. Despite all of this I still had *hope* in my heart. I was convinced that Easter was just around the corner. This was faith at its darkest, but it was faith at its strongest. If there could possibly be any highlight in such horrendous conditions, it was when Jesus entrusted his friend John to me. I felt certain, right there, that John represented every friend that Jesus would have until the end of time. Since that moment, my family has continued to grow! And *you*, my child, are a very special member of that very special group.

You can imagine, but have no real idea, just how I felt on Easter Sunday morning. I was in ecstasy. I live with that moment to this very day. Straightaway I became conscious of something wonderful … *Jesus' real work was only beginning now*, and I was going to have a special role to play in it. Nothing could have made me happier. The poor apostles needed all the 'mothering' I could give them, as they reassembled after running away and deserting him a few days earlier. I knew that this was part of their preparation, because unless they had a deep and personal conviction of their own weakness and powerlessness, the Holy Spirit could do little with them. It was part of my role to prepare them for Pentecost. And now, before we finish today, I'll give you a chance for a question or two.

I often wonder how you succeeded in keeping the apostles in that room for nine days, without anything happening. I think of Peter as getting very impatient if there was little action around. I can imagine Thomas asking for proof, *or he was quitting! To their minds, they had lost everything on Calvary. It was great for a while when Jesus returned to them, but now he was gone again, and all they had was a promise. I don't think they were very good at living on promises.*

Oh, how right you are! The one thing that helped was that they were very broken men, and they had the wind knocked out of their sails. It may not have been humility, but it was enough to go on with. Without realising it, they were profoundly impressed by how I dealt with Calvary, and all it entailed, and that gave me a slight advantage over them. They might not be too ready to take second place to a woman but, in this case, they had no choice. I went out of my way to assure and reassure them; to allay their fears, and to confirm their calling. To put it very simply, I told them that the Spirit would come because he was *expected*. In other words, 'we're staying here till he comes'! I settled that question right at the start. Then I lead them in quiet prayer, and soon our hearts and minds became united in prayer. This was a wonderful healing for them, and it helped them enormously. We were not counting the days, knowing that God is not bound by time and space. Jesus promised to send the Spirit, and that is all we needed to know. The Spirit was going to come, and we would be there to receive him. I spoke to them about the Spirit, and about my own experience of him. I spoke to them of the presence of the Spirit at all the great moments of birth in the history of the world. I spoke about the Spirit being there at the beginning of creation, and about how he brought order out of chaos. I spoke to them about the Spirit coming upon Jesus, and upon myself, at the beginning of our respective missions. I told them that it made all the sense in the world that the Spirit should come at this extraordinary moment, when Jesus' kingdom was about to be launched, and his message proclaimed. They listened, and they believed. The coming of the Spirit was a most extraordinary event. There was no doubt about what was happening. We had visual and audible evidence, and I was thrilled to see the tongue of fire resting on the head of each of the apostles. I feel that this was to remove for all time any lingering doubts they may have had. They could never deny what they saw and what they heard. Nor could they ever forget how they felt at that moment. They wanted to rush out the door, and convert the world! I held them in place for as long as I could, but soon I realised that their mission could begin immediately. Just as the stone had been rolled away from the tomb before Jesus emerged on Easter morning, so the doors of that Upper Room were flung open, and a group of highly powered and motivated men were released on the world. It was the beginning of the church. I don't have time today to tell you any more, but we will return to this on many occasions on other days. I pray for you, and I thank you for listening. I am so thrilled that you are to me what any one of those apostles was to me in that Upper Room.

CHAPTER FOUR

The Church

Here we go again. There are so many things I want to share with you, but I just will have to choose and select and, hopefully, cover most, if not all of them. I now want to share about church, because that was what emerged from Pentecost Sunday. On that day, the church was a small group of people, anointed and empowered by the Spirit, whose mission it was to tell the world the good news of the resurrection of Jesus. If Jesus had not risen from the dead, his mission would have been a failure, and there would be nothing to speak about to others. Imagine three large padlocked steel doors along a corridor. There is no way you can possibly escape from that building. Jesus broke down the first one (sin). He then broke down the second one (sickness). There is one left (death), and this is the strongest and most difficult one to take on. In fact, it was never thought that anyone could ever open this door, and allow safe passage through death into a life of eternal glory. When Jesus broke through that third door, he opened the way for all of us, *and it was essential that people be told that*. That is the reason for the church. During his life on earth, Jesus went around teaching and doing certain things. It was the responsibility of the apostles to continue this work, to complete this work. When Jesus did what he had to do, he returned in triumph to the Father, and he sent the Holy Spirit to complete his work on earth. A spirit, however, cannot *do* anything. An evil spirit needs somebody's tongue to tell the lie, or somebody's hand to plant the bomb. It is the same with the Holy Spirit. The Holy Spirit needs somebody's tongue to speak the word, or somebody's hands to be laid on the sick. Not that the Holy Spirit wants you to heal anybody. Only God can heal. The Spirit wants you to provide the hands and he will provide the power.

The next point is very important, and I will do my best to explain it to you as simply as I can. St Paul was not with Jesus, as the other apostles were. He was determined to crush the infant church, and he set out to do so. After he fell off his horse on the way to Damascus, he heard a voice saying, 'Saul, Saul (his name before he became a Christian) why do you persecute me?' 'Who are you Lord?' Saul asked. 'I am Jesus whom you are persecuting.' From that moment Saul (Paul) thought of 'Jesus' and 'church' as being the same thing. That is why he called the church 'the Body of Christ'. That is how I had to accept my role as Mother of the church. I was involved in giving birth to the church in that Upper Room at Pentecost. Jesus has come among us in various forms. The most common one is that of a baby in Bethlehem. After Pentecost, he remains on with his people in what we call the Body of Christ, or the church. And then, of course, he is present to his people in the Eucharist and, outside the times for Eucharist, he is still with them in every tabernacle in the world. Surely, at this stage, you must have some question?

Yes, indeed, I have. It must have been an extraordinary transformation that took place in the apostles that sent them out to face the world, and preach the gospel. Were you ever afraid for them, and what did you do to encourage them?

God's grace builds on nature; it does not replace it. What I mean by that is, no matter what power propelled them, they were still very weak human beings, and they could easily forget where their power came from. Jesus said, however, that 'the Holy Spirit *will remind you* of all I have said to you.' They needed those constant reminders. I tried my best to influence them, more by example than by words. What helped greatly was how the promises of Jesus began to come true for them. After his very first sermon, Peter converted three thousand people to become believers. Those who believed were baptised and added to the church. They joined with the other believers, and devoted themselves to the apostles' teaching and fellowship, sharing in the

Lord's Supper and in prayer. A great sense of awe came over them all, and the apostles performed many miraculous signs and wonders. And all the believers met together constantly, and shared everything they had. They sold their possessions, and shared the proceeds with those in need. They worshipped together at the Temple each day, met in homes for the Lord's Supper, and shared their meals with great joy and generosity – all the while praising God, and enjoying the goodwill of all the people. And each day the Lord added to their numbers those who were being saved. How grateful and happy I was to be able to share those early years with the emerging church. The apostles didn't need very much encouragement. They needed restraint more than encouragement, because they seem to have been freed from the fears that had crippled them for so long. It was glorious to watch the transformation that took place in them.

The end came very quietly for me. I was tired, and I just fell asleep. When I woke up I found myself in the presence of the Trinity. What a welcome All of Them had for me. Jesus still had the wounds, but they were dazzling with brilliance, and his face showed a love that I had never dreamed of. It soon became clear to me that there was going to be no sitting around here! Each of the Persons of the Trinity were very heavily involved in their work for their people. Jesus had promised his disciples that he would not leave them orphans, and so they had a Father, and they had me as a Mother. The variable was that they had to become like children, if God's plan was to work. God told Adam and Eve that he would send a woman who would crush the head of Satan. I discovered that I was that woman! I also discovered that Satan was determined to kill my baby once he was born. God did not permit this, so Satan switched his plans to destroy me. I was also preserved from his malice, so he declared war on all my children. When Satan was cast down to earth it was my role to preserve and safeguard my children. This role was a familiar one for me. Nazareth was a bleak barren desert, with snakes and vipers sliddering through the shrubs and the sand. I remember well that I didn't dare let the boy Jesus out of my sight, because of the dangers that surrounded him. I was now entrusted with a similar mission for all of God's children. For example, *you* are very precious to me, and I cast my mantle over you to protect you at all times.

It's extraordinary the way my role has never really changed at all in so many ways. I am still looking after Jesus, in the form of his church, the Body of Christ. I see the clouds of war gathering just as I saw the threats that were being mounted against him. Just as I always believed that Jesus was safe, and was always under the constant eye of the Father, so I believe today that the church will survive all attacks. The church has been going through a time of great purification for some time now, and this is not yet complete. Many of my children became discouraged, and feared that all would collapse, and the church would be overcome. I know well that, if they had stood with me on Calvary, they would have no reason to fear today. It is just history repeating itself. On a human level, Calvary was a disaster and a total failure. To some of the disciples, it was the end of the road, when all their dreams and hopes were shattered, and they felt very vulnerable indeed. It is so difficult for those of little faith to stand firm amidst the gales and the storms. Again and again Jesus said to his apostles 'Why did you doubt, oh you of little faith?' They had failed to learn one basic and simple lesson. Evil can *never* triumph, even if it is seen to have the upper hand for a while. Because of Jesus, even death itself has lost its victory. Satan *is* defeated but, because of his pride, he will battle on till the end of time to destroy the plans of God. The tragedy is that some people do fall for his lies, and he succeeds in leading them down a road that leads to eternal damnation. This breaks my heart, but I cannot stop anyone who is bent on self-destruction. Supposing you knew someone who was thinking of dying by suicide. You can talk as much as you like, you can watch out as much as is possible, and you may feel that you are being successful, but if that person is determined enough, death by suicide will surely happen.

I presume you are going to say something about scandals in the church, and the condition of the church today?

Yes, indeed, I am, because I consider it very important that you understand what is happening, and that you continue to hold your nerve, and live in faith and hope, as you stand with me and with the Holy Father on Calvary. Satan is extremely cunning, and he is quite capable of fooling and deceiving any of God's children, if I were not there to protect them. Sometimes his work is quite evident; at other times it is silent and unseen. Members of the church suffered great pain in recent years when the hidden scandals were revealed. Let me stress something straightaway. If the church is to be renewed, then every hidden scandal and wrong-doing must be exposed to the light of truth. It is like lancing a boil, so that all the puss and poison can be removed. Satan loves the cover-up, and those who cover-up the wrongs of others, at the expense of the innocent, are guilty of a greater crime than the original guilty party. That is why no stone should be left unturned, and no possible abuse should go unexamined until the truth, the whole truth, and nothing but the truth, is exposed to public view. Those of faith have no reason to fear, and that includes those who are guilty of wrong-doing. Being exposed to public accountability may well be the only way that such a one will face the truth, repent of the wrong-doing, and experience the love and forgiveness of God. What peace can such a one have if he is dreading a knock on the door, or a tap on the shoulder? Many of these wrong-doers are victims themselves, and even if they end up in a state prison, they have already spent long days and nights in a very dark prison of their own making. Quite often, the state prison is freedom, because a burden has been lifted, and they have time and opportunity to repent, to make amends, and to walk the Way.

Speaking of the Way reminds me that the name given to the first group of believers was 'Followers of the Way'. The title 'Christian' was a derogatory title given the early church in Antioch, but it is the one that stuck. It is no harm to think of the church as 'Followers of the Way', 'a group of believers', or, indeed, as Christians or other Christs. The only reason for the existence of the church is to proclaim the message of Jesus, and to announce the good news of his victory. For example, anyone who has really grasped the core message of the gospel would not be despondent with what's happening the church today. A Christian is someone with eternal *hope*. The only *real* sin you can commit, as a Christian, is not to have hope. If you had stood with me on Calvary, I would have been whispering to you about the hope and the promise of Easter. 'Don't worry. Easter is only around the corner.' Jesus said that, and I believed him. He said that the sin of this world was unbelief in him. He also said 'When the Son of Man comes will he find any faith on this earth?' Elizabeth told me that 'all of this happened to you because you *believed* the promises made you by the Lord.' This is my prayer for you, my beloved child. Please believe, despite the prophets of gloom and doom, that the church will survive, and all will be well. Over the years, I have watched and prayed as I saw the church pass through many crises. On each occasion God sent a 'Moses' to lead the church out of darkness and slavery. The present Holy Father is a very special child of mine, and he *knows* that all is well, and all manner of things will be well. His predecessor, the much beloved John Paul II, had the faith and the trust to hold the rudder firmly, and know that 'this too shall pass'.

Throughout history, I have found it necessary to intervene in the journey of my children. In Lourdes, Fatima, and Medjugorje, I have come in person to allay the fears of my children. I could not remain silent while my children found themselves in darkness, and the evil one seemed to have overcome the good. My children have responded with great generosity, and such places have become sources of many and great blessings for them. It is my on-going mission to 'rally the troops', and to oppose the evil one in every way possible. Especially do I remind them that 'my Immaculate Heart will finally triumph.' Things may have seemed disastrous on Calvary, but now I *know*. I no longer have to live on faith, because I can see things clearly now, and I know that the gates of hell cannot prevail against the church. The church is Jesus, in another form, and I know that he is now beyond the slings and arrows of men. He died once, and his resurrection guaranteed victory for all eternity. Even though I suffer to see my children suffering, and my Mother's heart yearns for everyone to heed the words and promises of Jesus, yet I have no reason for despair. As at Cana, I repeat 'Do whatever he tells you', and I know that you will have your miracle. In all of the many places and times when I have intervened, and spoken directly to some of my children, I have never said anything that was not a repeat of the message of Jesus. I cannot, nor do I want to usurp his position in the order of things. It is at his bidding that I act. He still treats and honours me as a mother, and he knows that I love the church as much as I have ever loved him. Nothing really has changed for me, as my original mission still continues in another form. When Jesus chose to take on human nature, it meant being born of a mother, and behaving towards that mother as he would wish all children to behave towards their own mothers. Even now, in heavenly glory, with all authority in heaven and on earth entrusted to him, he has chosen not to change his relationship with me. This is a humbling experience for me, but I just have to accept that this is how he wishes things to be. I am privileged and delighted to be able to pour out graces and blessings on all of my children, and this gives great joy to his heart too. Like a mother of any family, I long for unity and belonging among my children. It pains me to see division and strife among my children, but I know that this will all be healed in time. I long for the day when there will be one fold and one shepherd, and my Son will be acknowledged as Lord in his kingdom. This kingdom is a safe place for his children, and it is his wish (and mine) that more and more people become willing to live within the security of that kingdom. In that kingdom Jesus is Lord; his word is our guidance to peace and happiness. Every one of his children is equal in his sight, and he wants each one to receive and to enjoy equal rights. And, finally, the power to live in that kingdom is solely the work of the Holy Spirit. The kingdom, the power, and the glory are his; not yours, not mine. My only wish and longing is to proclaim his message, and to protect his children. Nothing gives me greater joy that this.

If I might come in here with a question, please. It doesn't look like the whole world is prepared to march to the tune of 'Onward Christian Soldiers'. Do you not think, in a way, the task is impossible? After all, the apostles went out to convert the world, to preach the good news to all nations, and now, two thousand years later, the Christian message has not, and is not making a great impact on the world. At this present time, for example, Islam seems to be the religion that is spreading like a forest fire across the globe, just as one would hope that the Christian message would evoke such enthusiasm, and such a response? What's the difference, really, and does it make much difference which religion I belong to, as long as I belong to God, and worship him?

Let me say straightaway that God has no grandchildren; we are *all* children of God. The division into the separate religions was the work of people, not of God. The message of the gospel cannot be divided, altered, or made to suit the needs and fantasies of certain people. However, because many of these people are very sincere, and genuinely want to serve God, they are totally accepted by God just as they are. God is not very interested in the external 'trappings' of religion. When the woman at the well argued with Jesus about whether it was better to worship God in the Temple, or on the mountain, he told her that a time would come when it would not matter where we worshipped God, as long as we did so in spirit and in truth. Jesus died for *all* peoples, whether they know that or not. No one is going to be penalised because they have never heard that good news. The role of the church is to be a light to the world. One candle can effect the darkness in a whole room. Jesus tells you that *you* are the light of the world, and the salt of the earth. You are asked to light a candle, rather than complain about the darkness. Salt gives taste, and it also preserves. Without salt, many foods would go bad, and not last till their 'sell by' date. It is said that one rotten apple can cause all the others to go bad. The opposite to that is that one committed Christian can generate and promote goodness among the whole community. Again, Jesus refers to the effect of a little yeast on a whole basin of flour. You might well wonder just what good the church is doing in the world. One of the ways of testing this (which is frightening) is to remove the church entirely, and see what happens to the world then. The unity of the human and the divine that took place in Jesus would be missing, and religion would revert to a set of rules, regulations, and commandments, just as Jesus found it among the Pharisees. People of *all* religions and of none cannot but hear the voice of the Holy Father, of Mother Teresa, or of Padre Pio. They may differ in their beliefs, but they are united in their admiration. What I speak about here is the *witness* value of the church. 'You shall be my witnesses until the ends of the earth,' Jesus had told his apostles. There is one mistake that has consistently been made throughout history, and it continues right to this day. The church tends to emphasise *uniformity* rather than *unity*. Uniformity is when we all goose-step out the door together, to the beat of the same drum. For example, some years ago it was a sin to eat meat on Fridays. This rule applied to all Catholics, even though many of them were so poor that they never had the luxury of meat and, if they were fortunate enough to get some, they had to be careful what day of the week it was! Like any loving mother, I rejoice in the differences and uniqueness of each of my children. 'Cloning' is a word that has very dangerous and potentially evil connotations. Unity is about being united in heart and spirit because, no matter whether it is Buddha or Mohammed, they all worship the same God. The Christian message continues to have a profound influence on the world, even among those who do not belong. The role of the church is to continue to give witness, to struggle for peace and justice, and never to count heads. If Jesus required that everyone be ready to listen to him, he would not have started yet! As a Christian, you have a clear and definite message, with sure and certain promises. You have witnessed the lives of real saints even during your own lifetime. I am happy that the church 'canonises' its saints, because it helps to remind you that you are all called to be saints, even if only some of you get canonised. Never before in the history of the world have so many 'angels' walked among you. Thérèse of Lisieux, Faustina, Mother Teresa, Padre Pio, John Paul II, to mention but a few from a very long list. If you belong to such an illustrious group, then you can feel secure in belonging. There is enormous holiness and goodness in today's church, and this gives great joy to my heart. You are part of that church; you are part of that joy. Thank you. Thank you.

CHAPTER FIVE

Eucharist

When I speak about Eucharist, I speak about what you normally call the 'Mass', and what you also call 'The Blessed Sacrament', which is Jesus present in the tabernacle. I want to share with you what I think of this, so that your own understanding will have greatly increased. It is difficult to grasp the real meaning and significance of the Mass if you were not on Calvary. If you stood with me on Calvary, you would have seen the ugliness of sin, the extraordinary depth of God's forgiveness, and the extent Jesus had to go in saying his *Yes* to the Father, before the *No* of Adam and Eve could be wiped away. It is as if sin was nailed to the cross with Jesus, so that when he died, sin would also have to die. It was a struggle unto death with the evil one. It may seem a contradiction, but Satan did everything within his power to *prevent* Jesus from dying! Satan knew that if Jesus' obedience could bring him all the way to death, then there was no hope of ever defeating him. His *Yes* was total, and unconditional. When Peter tried to persuade Jesus not to go up to Jerusalem, because of the dangers awaiting him there, Jesus knew what was behind it, and he replied, 'Get behind me, Satan.' Peter was a good man, and he loved Jesus very much, and he would never have believed that Satan could speak through him. Peter was also a weak man and, when the pressure began to grow, he lost his nerve and ran. I longed for Peter to be with me on Calvary. I longed for all the apostles to be there. If they were, they would have witnessed Jesus at his most powerful, when he was nailed to a cross, and could do nothing, *because that is where the Father wanted him to be*. In spite of the pain and suffering, Calvary was an extraordinary place. The whole history of the world was being reversed there, and the whole future of mankind was being determined. There was a tangible sense of God's presence, as well as the stench of the evil one. Jesus was saying *Yes* to the Father, on behalf of all of God's children. My special friends were gathered around me, as we tried to add our *Yes* to his. The Jewish people were used to sacrifices, but this was the greatest sacrifice ever offered, and very few were aware of that. This was the Lamb of God, of which the sacrifice of other lambs over the centuries was but a shadow. His precious blood dripped onto the ground and soaked into it. This would make the earth sacred for all time. Yes, you have a question?

Yes, when you spoke of the earth becoming sacred, I was thinking of the way we are treating the earth today, through pollution, pesticides, and artificial growth promoters. Many of the forests are being destroyed, and the rivers being polluted, so soon there will be no safe place for the birds or the fish. What do you think of this?

While I don't want to be distracted from speaking about Calvary, I just have to give you an answer to that. Greed drives people to get money *at all costs*, and they are totally disinterested in what is happening to the environment. Selfishness enables them to put their wealth before their own children, who will inherit a climate that is badly damaged, and an environment that will not be conducive to good health. All I want to say, for now, is that this is *wrong, wrong, wrong.* On the positive side, there are many good and generous people who are aware of what is happening, and who care about this. They are doing their utmost to draw attention to the destruction of the earth, and they are calling on others to join them in a crusade to stop the destruction, before it is too late. I'm sure I will have a chance later on to return to this subject but, for now, I am anxious to return to the scene on Calvary.

Talking about the earth, the moment of Jesus' death was one of violent upheaval for earth and sky. The sky went dark, and the earth trembled. The graves opened, and gave up their dead.

The buildings shook, and the veil in the Temple, that separated the people from the Holy of Holies, was torn in two. It was as if God was telling the people that, from now on, they could come right into his presence. I drew on every word that Jesus ever spoke, and on my own deep expectations and hope, as I struggled to comfort and assure my friends. My heart was pierced like the nails in Jesus' body, and the only real difference between us was the blood. My tears mingled with his blood, as it fell upon me, while I clung to the cross. I tried to be as close to him as I could, and I was grateful that the soldiers did not deprive me of this unique privilege. It was necessary that I share this time as much as was possible, because Jesus would entrust to me the responsibility of telling future generations about it. For the sake of simplicity, from here on, when I speak about the Mass I will use the word Eucharist, and this will remain separate from the Real Presence of Jesus in the tabernacle. If my children are to understand Eucharist, then they have to understand Calvary. On Calvary, Jesus said his *Yes* to the Father. At Eucharist, you join your *Yes* to his *Yes* to the Father. Calvary happened just once, but the *Yes*, the prayer of Calvary, can be repeated until the end of time.

I know that you were on Calvary, but do you have any role to play in the Eucharist? Are you present with the people during Eucharist?

A very good question, and I'm delighted you asked it. I am present at every Eucharist that is offered throughout the world. I would love to hear the following prayer from the hearts of those present, before Eucharist begins 'Mary, my Mother, please come with me to the altar, and help me join my *Yes* to Jesus, to his *Yes* to the Father.' I stand at the altar at each celebration of Eucharist, just as I did on Calvary. My joy is that I have many more with me than I had then.

Please understand that Calvary had to do with sin, forgiveness, reconciliation, and a complete return of his people to the family of God. When you begin Eucharist, you call to mind your sins, and you ask for forgiveness. Lest you forget why you're there, you hear these words at the consecration: 'which is shed for you and for all for the forgiveness of sins'. And again, at Communion, you are told: 'This is the Lamb of God who takes away the sins of the world.' There is no way we can afford, nor will we be allowed to forget, the connection between Calvary/ Eucharist and our sinful state. Bread and wine were central to the stable diet of people in Jesus' time on earth. His first miracle had to do with wine, and he multiplied bread on more than one occasion to feed his hungry followers. When he wanted us to understand his role, he spoke of himself as the Bread of Life. We make these gifts available, and we ask the Holy Spirit to do the rest. ('Let Your Holy Spirit come upon them, that they may become for us the Body and Blood of Our Lord Jesus Christ.') You may wonder how you would have acted had you being present with me on Calvary. Each time you are present at Eucharist, you have an opportunity to discover how you would have been. Approach each celebration as if it were your *first* time, as if it were your *last* time, as if it were your *only* time to be present at such an extraordinary privilege. If you knew what a privilege it is to be present at Eucharist, you would avail of every opportunity you get to be there.

The prayers used during Eucharist are very significant. You begin by being nourished by the Word of God in the readings and homily, and you end by being nourished by the Bread of Life, the Body and Blood of Jesus himself. You share in the unique privilege that was mine, when Jesus comes to live within you. Just as I brought Jesus to visit Elizabeth, so you can bring him to touch the lives of those you meet, either through the words you say, the prayers you pray, the life you live, or the very person that you are. There are prayers for the church, for the holy souls, and the souls in glory are also invoked; all of which is to give you a much wider canvas, and to emphasise that the Eucharist is being offered for the *world*, and to give thanks and praise to God. The word 'Eucharist' means 'Thanks', and it is a mistake to think that you should always have an 'intention' when you offer this sacrifice to God. It is a mistake to always be *asking* for something, because this turns the attention to yourself, rather than giving God your full attention. There are some of my children who offer Eucharist, especially on Saturdays, for *my* intentions, and this pleases me very much. By doing this they are joining me in praying for so many needs in today's world that are so evident to me. I need you to help me in my mission, and all those faithful children of mine who share my mission are a source of great joy to me. Some of them are like my 'recruiting sergeants', who are constantly calling others to respond to my call for the welfare of the world.

Before you receive Eucharist, you join with others in calling God 'Father', and you turn to the others with a sign of peace. This is highly significant. Jesus said that 'if you bring your gift to the altar, and there remember that your brother has something against you, leave your gift at the altar, go and be reconciled with your brother, and then come and offer your gift'. Eucharist is about building *community*, the Body of Christ. At Communion, the Body of Christ (community) is being nourished by the Body of Christ (Communion). It saddens me to see Eucharist celebrated where there is absolutely no interaction between the people present, or indeed, between the priest and the people. Eucharist should give *witness* to belonging, to becoming, to being part of a family, or community. When you come in the door of the church, you come from different situations and conditions, and you may not be very conscious of having much in common with the other people who are gathering. By the time Eucharist has ended, you should have a strong sense of being *one* with the rest of the congregation, and you should go out the door, encouraged and strengthened by that experience.

I would like you to go back to Calvary for a while, because it seems to me that that is the only way that I am ever going to appreciate what the Eucharist is about, and how I can best participate in it.

Very good. I am delighted to do that. I could speak to you about

Calvary all day long, and never tire, nor exhaust the subject. I can imagine, when you were young, that you fancied yourself standing right there beside me at the foot of the cross. That is a sure sign of your goodwill, but it may not be too realistic. On a human level, Calvary was a total disaster, and for the on-looking unbeliever, it must have appeared that Jesus was totally defeated. When God first created people, he had planned that they should be with him for all eternity. Death was not part of his plan. When Adam and Eve fell for the lie, however, it was as if the human race came under new management. They walked away from the light and the truth and, because they had severed the cord uniting them to God, they had lost the prospect of eternal life. They were human, of course, but, after original sin, they became mortal. A mortal being will die, as will each and everything he/she accomplishes. God came up with a most extraordinary plan to turn things around, one that must be very obvious to the blindest of human beings. He would come down among them, take on their human condition, and *die*. He would then rise from the dead, and appear among them again. They should see, beyond all question or doubt that he had overcome death, and it would no longer be an enemy for them. 'Dying you destroyed our death; rising, you restored our life' are words with which you are familiar. *Eucharist is a celebration of that victory.* Eucharist differs from Calvary in so far as it contains the 'whole package' of death and resurrection. Each of my children can attend Eucharist, and be united with me in all that happened on Calvary and on Easter morning. I welcome those who join me at Bethlehem, but there is a much greater possibility involved in Easter. Look at a crucifix, and keep looking at it, until you let it imprint itself on your mind and heart. The longer you spend looking at that crucifix, the more aware you will become of the price that Jesus paid for your freedom. I cannot accept that you can properly enter into the spirit of Easter if you have not been steeped in the event of Good Friday. When you come to Eucharist, you *have* to become personally involved in all that happens there. It is so easy to just sit back, and let the priest get on with it. It is so easy to hold the priest responsible for whether the Eucharist is 'good' or not. What a mistake that is! If the priest was deaf and dumb, and reading the prayers in total silence in his own mind, this takes not one iota from the extraordinary power of that Eucharist. If the priest said the prayers in Chinese, or if he is old, confused, and repeating the prayers, it takes nothing whatever from your responsibility to share fully in the sacrifice of Calvary. The conditions that prevailed on that first Good Friday made it almost impossible for my friends who were with me to pray. I had to encourage them by example, and become as united as was possible to the prayer being offered by Jesus. There is *nothing* that could prevent you from saying your *Yes*, if you choose to do so. You asked me to say a few extra words about Calvary, and I hope that what I have said will help you. While you are present at Eucharist, I look upon you as someone who stood by my side on Calvary all those years ago. I thank you for that from the bottom of my heart. You are very special to me indeed.

Each celebration of Eucharist is different. The Feastdays change, the readings change, and the vestments change. In the course of a year, you are brought through so much of the scriptures, and you celebrate so much of what is special in the story of your salvation. You honour me in several Feastdays, and you honour those special people whom you call the saints. Most especially, of course, the liturgical year brings you through the life, death, resurrection, and ascension of Jesus. This is repeated year after year, as if you were spinning around in a washing machine. You are being washed, purified, and restored to your original beauty when God first created a human being. It is said that 'familiarity breeds contempt (or content?)' That is the greatest danger for those who attend Eucharist regularly. It is even more dangerous for the priest, who runs the risk of reducing and seeing the Eucharist as something he has to 'perform', where the emphasis is on 'getting through it'. This really breaks my heart. You can imagine the joy I experienced as I stood beside St Padre Pio during Eucharist. Oh, what a tragedy and travesty that it should be reduced to just going through the motions. Such a Eucharist is better not being said. Jesus died only once, but the prayer of that death can be offered every single day. Remember, you are not offering your own prayer; rather are you joining your prayer with his and, indeed, with mine. It is my heartfelt wish that both priest and congregation might give some time beforehand to reflecting on why they are there, and what they expect should happen there. You must surely enter the door of the church on occasions when your mind is in turmoil, your blood is boiling with anger, and your body is weary and listless. How can you expect to enter into the spirit of Eucharist if that is how you are? Come in the door by all means, oh, please do. But before you begin to open your spirit to why you are there, you should turn to me, tell me how you feel, and ask me to accompany you to the altar. That is a prayer that I will delight in answering, a prayer that I could never refuse. You have come to the right place, but your attitude will have to be adjusted if you are to benefit from the infinite blessings that are available. Jesus would never apologise for his preference for the poor, the broken, and the outcasts. 'He welcomed sinners, and even ate with them.' In one way, you would be an ideal client to be present at Eucharist. (Please excuse the smile!) However, if you are not prepared to change, then you will bring all your hurts home with you, because Jesus is prevented from healing you. He only heals those who *want* to be healed, and are prepared to ask him, and allow him to heal them. 'Do you want to be healed?' he asked the man at the pool. He never went around healing people, nor does he do so today. He went around (and still does) with the *power* to heal, and the person along the roadside has to make a decision. Otherwise, Jesus will not stop, but will simply pass by. 'Jesus of Nazareth is passing by', were the words that the blind Bartimeus heard. He began to call out, and continued to call, until Jesus stopped and healed him. Let me ask you a simple question. If Eucharist is what I say it is, should you be surprised if someone is healed while being present? I know that many would be amazed if this happened, whereas I wish that they should become amazed that it doesn't happen! Surely all the conditions for healing can easily be present in the course of celebrating Eucharist. Several of the prayers speak about health of mind and body, and Jesus is asked to 'say but the word, and I shall be healed'.

I know about Confession, or the Sacrament of Reconciliation, but would you say that sin can be forgiven during the celebration of Eucharist?

Thank you for asking that question. Oh, how I wish that people would realise just how much Eucharist can be involved in the forgiveness of sin. The problem began many years ago, when Mass and Confession became tied in with each other, and you couldn't have one without the other. Your parents grew up with the belief that they had to go to Confession on Saturday before they could go to Communion on Sunday. This is something that has greatly damaged the whole *celebration* of both sacraments. Hopefully, in a later session together, I will get to share with you about reconciliation. It has a place, of course, a very special place. But it must *never* be confused with Eucharist. If 'going to Confession' is intended to make yourself 'worthy' of going to Communion, then I have bad news for you! You will *never* be worthy of Eucharist, no matter how much you try. You come in the door of that church with all your faults, failings, and hungers. You confess your sins, and ask for forgiveness. You strike your breast, and confess that you are not worthy. You are invited to receive the 'Lamb of God who takes away the sins of the world'. Surely, after all of that, do you still doubt that your sins are forgiven? It is very difficult to define *serious sin*, but suffice it to say that it separates us from God, and requires sincere and humble confession on our part, through the Sacrament of Reconciliation, before I am reconciled with God and with myself. It may also involve making reconciliation with some other person as well. For the ordinary person, however, who has enough goodwill to be present at Eucharist, surely all the ingredients are there for the forgiveness of anything that Jesus sees is in need of forgiveness. Rather than look for forgiveness by some other means, just come to Eucharist as you are, and allow Jesus to wash you in his Precious Blood, which 'is shed for you and for many for the forgiveness of sins'.

There is so much more I would love to share with you about Eucharist, but I'll have to stop for now. If you remember *some* of what I have told you, and especially that I really long to go with you to the altar to help you add your *Yes* to Jesus, to his *Yes* to the Father, then you are on a learning curve that will lead you into the very heart of this extraordinary gift. Thank you for listening. You make me so happy.

CHAPTER SIX

Prayer

It gives me great joy to share with you how I see prayer, and what I consider it to be. So as not to complicate things, when I speak of prayer, I am not speaking of *saying* prayers. The organ that God gave you with which to pray is the *heart*, not the tongue. If the heart is not praying, then the tongue is wasting its time. Prayer is many things. It involves 'spending time' with God, just as you are spending time with me now. Spending time with the other is a very important part of any friendship and, without that, it is impossible for a relationship to grow. There is no question of *achieving* anything in prayer, as if God was counting your prayers and doling out Brownie points, according as you delivered. If you spend time with God, you can be sure that God won't be idle. He is the Creator, and he never stops creating. This applies to all forms of prayer, no matter to whom the prayers are addressed. I said 'prayers addressed' and, lest this gives the impression that prayer is saying things, I want to stress that some of the most meaningful prayer takes place in total silence. To help 'tidy' this up a bit, I will stay with *vocal* prayers for a while. The attitude you bring to such a time is more important than anything you have to say. Check that you are in a proper 'prayer mode'. What I mean by this is that you stand before heaven *exactly as you are seen from there*. Remember there is no point in pretending, excusing, denying, or blaming. You are X-rayed in all of your being, and the *real you* is what is showing on the big screen in heaven. Make sure that you tune into this before you open your mouth. (This same condition applies to all forms of prayer, of course.) When you are prepared to stand before heaven, exactly as you are, knowing that there is nothing

hidden, then you are ready to put in words what you may have
in your heart. This could be praise or thanks, contrition or peti-
tion. *Know* that you are heard, and know that such a privilege is
an answer in itself. Prayer of praise is the highest form of prayer.
It is the prayer of the angels and saints in heaven. There are
many many ways of praising God, and I will speak about most
of them during our time together today. I am anxious to avoid
confusion and, therefore, when I speak of prayer I am including
you pouring out your heart to God, in any of his Persons, to me,
or to any of the angels and saints. Once a prayer is directed to
heaven, we all hear it. It is if we were allowed to read each
other's mail! The answer to all prayer, and the blessings for all
prayer, come from God anyhow, no matter who else speaks on
your behalf. Oh, if you only knew how many friends you have
here in the heavenly court. There are so so many who are delighted to listen, and take care of your prayer, if you choose to
approach them. Don't worry, there is no competition, there is no
popularity poll. We are all conduits of graces and blessing from
God, and all that we ask is that God be glorified, and you are
blessed. When I speak about saying prayers, I am not thinking of
any particular prayers that you may recite at some particular
time. I am speaking about vocal prayer in general. All I ask is
that you get yourself into the right 'mode' as you stand before
heaven. If you understood what that really meant, I don't think
there would be any muttering, or any great rush to get them
'over'. If you *really* understood what is implied, it would be very
easy indeed to pour out your heart, and to feel and know that
you are being heard.

*I know that the Holy Spirit has something to do with all forms of
prayer, and I would love to hear you speak about that.*

And I would certainly love to speak about that. I have surprised
myself that I got so far into today's session without even men-
tioning the Holy Spirit! I *live* by the power of the Spirit, and I
know that you depend greatly on him as well, so maybe I did

not see a great need for specific emphasis. Of course, we cannot exaggerate the central role the Holy Spirit plays in all forms of prayer. It is the Holy Spirit who turns your words into prayer. Without the Holy Spirit, you are just saying words, and they are going nowhere. It's like using a mobile phone with no battery in it. You can press as many buttons as you wish, but you'll never make contact at the other end. I suggest that you begin *all* prayer – and I mean *all* prayer – with a short prayer to the Holy Spirit. The words don't matter, but here's one version: 'Oh Holy Spirit, Breath and Power of God, I ask you please to be in my words to turn my words into prayer. Be in my heart as a Spirit of Truth that I may be sincere in what I say.'

There are many forms of prayer, but I will choose three forms, and deal with each in order. They are Vocal Prayers, Meditation, and Contemplation. Vocal prayers are the prayers you say, many of which you learned at your mother's knee. (The Rosary is one such prayer but, as you can imagine, I will require a whole session on its own for this.) You have prayers that you say in the morning, when you ask for help during the day, and you have prayers you say at night, when you give thanks for the day just ending. You may well have a prayerful spirit, and you whisper many prayers in the course of the day. Perhaps you pray together as a family. If you do, I would ask you to do something very important. Family prayer often includes people of different ages, and it can be difficult, if not impossible, to have all of them with the same mind-set when you come together to pray. Someone must take the lead, however, and ensure that, if you pray together, you do so with reverence and attention. Without this emphasis on the *quality* of the prayers, they will become faster and shorter in no time. When you pray on your own, you should remember that God weighs your prayers, rather than counting them. One Hail Mary said with reverence and attention is better than a whole Rosary that is rattled off, without much attention to what you're doing. To summarise what I want to say about vocal prayer: Begin with a prayer to the Holy Spirit, stand before heaven as you are seen in heaven, and speak your words with reverence, attention, and respect.

To simplify what I mean by Meditation I will limit it to your use of the gospels. When you think of the gospels, I want you to remember two things: The gospels are *now*, and *you* are every person in the gospels. You begin, as usual, with a short prayer to the Holy Spirit. Then you select a passage from one of the gospels, which can be an incident involving a miracle, or one of Jesus' teachings. You read it very slowly, once for the head, and a second time for the heart. You may have to read it more than twice before you are ready to become 'part' of it. When you are ready, and have made yourself comfortable, just close your eyes. Switch on the slide projector in your head, and use your creative imagination to try to visualise the scene right there in front of you. Make it as real as possible, identifying each person in the scene. Take as long as you wish for this, so that it begins to soak into your inner being. In your mind, you become part of that scene. You are sitting or standing in some particular spot. When you are ready, you can take the role, and play the role of the main character in the scene, e.g. the centurion, Jairus, the leper, etc. Jesus is as much present to you as he was to that person when that incident first happened. Make the prayer of the leper your own. Now that you have Jesus' attention, try to get a feeling of being in his presence, and of being within his healing touch. Spend as much time as you want at this, not always *asking* for things, but just looking, contemplating, and reflecting. You can be certain that Jesus is *really* present to you, just as I would be if you joined me at the Annunciation, Bethlehem, Cana, or Calvary. Yes, indeed, the gospels are *now*, and you are every person in them.

From what you say, my presence in that scene is more than just imaginary. I had never thought that I could actually be present at some event that happened 2,000 years ago!

Oh yes, you can! That's the secret of reading the gospels. They are *alive*. They are not just historical accounts of events, as you might read in a history book. That man/woman is *you*. When you enter in to the aliveness of the gospels, they begin to seep into your spirit, and you realise that you are part of the most extraordinary story ever told. In an earlier session, I asked you to *listen* to what Jesus says, and to *watch* what he does. By doing this, you will come to *know* him. What better way to come to know Jesus than through the gospels. Please never hesitate to ask me to be with you in each and every scene. I so much want you to absorb the gospels, and to make them alive. After all, you are asked to live them, and it is necessary to absorb them before that can become possible. I will speak about the Rosary later. All I want to say now is that the Rosary is greatly enriched by having you reflect on scenes from the gospels, as you recite the vocal prayers. It combines two methods of prayer.

There are so many other subjects for Meditation besides the gospel events. You can sit before Jesus in the Blessed Sacrament, use your creative imagination, and make the scene come alive. You close your eyes, and you imagine Jesus there in front of you. How is he dressed? What do you notice about his hair, or the colour of his skin? Is he sitting or standing? Will you go up to him, or will he come down to you? What do you want to say to him? Listen to what he is saying to you. Would you like to go for a walk with him across a nearby field? Sit on a rock together, and enjoy his company, just as he certainly enjoys yours. Do you have anybody at home or in hospital to whom you would love to bring him? Imagine walking down the hospital corridor with him, and get him a chair to sit by the bed of your friend. See his smile as he reaches out to place his hand on the head of the person who is sick. There is no limit to what you can experience if you are prepared to use your creative imagination. It is one of your greatest gifts for Meditation.

The third method of prayer I want to talk about is called Contemplation. This can be more difficult to understand. (In fact, it is impossible if you try it without invoking the inspiration and guidance of the Holy Spirit!) In the first two methods of prayer you were fairly active, either vocally, or with your imagination. In this method of prayer, you do nothing. When we come to Contemplation, we are entering into the very heart of prayer. Real prayer is what God does when you give him time and space. Only God can do a God-thing. By yourself you can say prayers, but you cannot pray. That is the work of the Spirit within you. In Contemplation you go down into your heart, down where you are most yourself, and it is there that you encounter the Spirit. This is a slow and beautiful *process*. Once you give time and space to it, the process will happen, and you will be able to spend long periods in simple Contemplation before the throne of God. You enter into the spirit by going through the body. In other words, you spend some time at the beginning becoming more and more aware of the body. You concentrate on your breathing … in … out … in … out. You focus on the heart, as you feel it pumping away, sending life around your body. You tense every muscle in your body, one after the other, and you relax each muscle as much as you possibly can. You follow one of your breaths right down into your inner being, and you stay down there. You remain still, and simply focus on being at the very core of your being. To help you stay down there, you pick a word ('mantra'), which you slowly repeat over and over again. It can be 'Jesus', 'Amen', 'Glory', etc. You feel a great peace descending upon you, and you seem to have located some sort of 'still point' within, where there is no need to act or to speak. In fact, words or actions would destroy the whole process. 'Be still and know that I am God.' You have a profound sense of being tiny, tiny, before the Face of Almighty God. 'At the centre of our being is a point of nothingness, which is untouched by sin and by illusion, a point of pure truth, a point or spark which belongs entirely to God. This little point of nothingness, and of absolute poverty, is the pure glory of God in us. It is like a pure diamond, blazing with the invisible light of heaven. It is in everybody, and if we could see it, we would see these millions of points of light coming together in the face and blaze of a sun that would make all the darkness and cruelty of life vanish completely.' (Thomas Merton) You are like a grain of sand on the seashore, and you have taken your proper place before God.

It is important that you *know* your place before God, because it is so easy to take over, and try to run the show yourself.

If I might interrupt you for a moment, but my big concern would be distractions. *I can't say a Hail Mary without being distracted! I'm not sure I would be a good subject for this Contemplation, because my mind is too scattered.*

Yes, indeed, join the human race! Contemplative prayer is a *gift*, and without the work of the Holy Spirit within, you will never make any headway. Pray, and ask for a contemplative spirit, and you will receive it. I certainly would be more than willing to answer such a prayer, because it is a beautiful request for a very necessary gift. Part of the process, or the journey, is a gradual handing over to God of all that concerns God. The first thing you have to do is stop playing God. As soon as you do that, God will take over, and he will have a free hand in filling your heart with his Spirit. I smiled when you asked about distractions, because I'm afraid they are going to continue to be part of all your prayers for a long time yet. Distractions are not 'bad'. Let me put it to you this way. You spend an hour in some attempt at Contemplation. During that hour, your mind wanders to what you did that morning, or what you have to do this evening. You wonder if you locked the car, or if you should go to the shops, in case you may not have enough bread for tea. Let's say that, in the course of that hour, your mind wandered sixty times. That's discouraging, and you feel that your prayer is a complete fail-ure. Do you know how God sees it? He knows that, in the course of one hour, your mind was distracted sixty times, but each time that happened *you turned back to him*. As far as God is concerned, you have had sixty successes! (Anyhow, who is counting?) I'm sure you know that, like everything else you ever learned, you will become better at it in time. To have the goodwill to make yourself available for such prayer, and to call upon the Holy Spirit to help and guide you, will surely lead to a real encounter with God, distractions or not. Contemplation is spending time with God, and what happens there is what he does. You cannot, therefore, have such a thing as 'failure'.

You can pray a lot, without saying many prayers. The secret here is to develop a praying heart. In other words, your heart can become a Prayer Room, a Pentecost Place, an Upper Room. This is a role which I am privileged to play in the lives of those who invite me. When I am allowed become the caretaker of your heart, I can obtain and supervise the miracle there. I will provide the conditions in which the Spirit works best, and I will pray in you, with you, and for you. I love to be invited to live within a human heart. I was gifted with a deep contemplative spirit. The gospels speak of me 'pondering all these things in her heart'. That is something that I love to cultivate within the hearts of all my children. Like any mother, I just love to help my children, and ensure that they grow into mature responsible followers of Jesus. Prayer nourishes the soul, and I want all of my children to be healthy and well. I am always alert, as I was at Cana, and I have no reason to hesitate going to Jesus for anything. He has given me that wonderful privilege, and I just love to use it for all that is best for my children.

One of the things that I want to stress before we finish today, is that prayer is actually very simple, and is quite pleasant and easy to engage in. Of course, if you approach it with clenched fists, gritted teeth, and flexed muscles, you are going to have a real endurance test indeed. If the heart is 'on-line', the prayer becomes spontaneous. A great deal depends on your inner attitude. If you do not appreciate God's love, and his blessings in your life, then you are going to have difficulty in praising and thanking him. It is not possible to be grateful and unhappy at the same time. You should check on your gratitude, because it really does effect your prayer – either for good or for bad. If I could bring you to show you an oasis in a desert, I could use it to explain something I want you to understand. Beneath the driest desert there is plenty of water, but it is a very rare place, indeed, where the water can rise to the surface. An oasis is a source of life to the people, the animals, and the birds. The trees and grass are in full growth, and it is a veritable heaven on earth to those who find it. Let's go back a mile or two, and examine the sand. It is dry and dusty; it is not possible to make a 'sandball' out of it, and nothing can grow in it. Sometimes prayer can be like an oasis, and other times it can be pure desert. It matters naught to God how we feel when we pray. The fact that we are willing to give him time and space is what really pleases him. When we spend time with him, we are working on our relationship with him. If you pray only when you *feel* like praying, you might not pray too much. Love is a *decision*, not a feeling. Prayer involves a decision, and that's what pleases God the most. When it comes to prayer he wants decisions, not discussions. Please allow me the unique privilege of being part of your prayer-life. Your earthly mother taught you your first prayers. Please allow me to continue the process, so that I can join you on the journey. There is nothing that would give me more pleasure.

In a later session, I will deal with the need of *your* prayers in today's world. If I can get enough of my children to respond to my call for prayer, the world can be saved from great disasters. I look forward to sharing this with you soon. For the present, thank you for your attention, and for your goodwill. You bring great joy to my heart.

CHAPTER SEVEN

I Need Your Prayers

When you looked at the title of today's session, you probably were taken by surprise. You may never have thought of me needing prayers. That is why I have to be extremely careful to present this to you in sure and certain language, and in a way that will leave you in no doubt whatever about what I have in mind. You cannot be living in the world today and not realise how many dangers are lurking. Surely it should not require any more genocides, atrocities, or huge natural disasters to convince people that all is not well. In the simple prayer that Jesus taught, you are to pray that God's will may be done on earth as it is in heaven. You don't have to go beyond the front page of your morning paper to know that this is not happening today. There is a corruptive and erosive influence working away at the fabric of society, and the world is becoming an unsafe place to live, where the accepted values and norms are completely against all that is good for my children. Right from the start, let me tell you the reality. You may remember, in an earlier session, when Satan failed to destroy me or my baby, that he declared war on the rest of my children. That is what is happening today. There is a spiritual arms-race on for the souls and hearts of people.

Excuse me, I'm sorry for coming in so soon, but I'm puzzled that God allows this to happen, and I am also amazed that you should need my help to do something that is away beyond my ability.

That's a very understandable question, and I will answer it as simply as I can. You *are* important in the eyes of God. He is not going to by-pass you as if you didn't exist, but he wants you to join in, and play a part in the salvation of the world. Remember you *never* have to supply the *power*. The kingdom, the power, and the glory are his. If you supply any of the power, you may be tempted to steal some of the glory! You see, it is *you* who is under attack. God is not defending himself. If I can only get you to join in the counterattack, that will not only strengthen you, but it will contribute to the eternal defeat of Satan. It is a wonderful plan of God to include you in his work. It is certainly my very strong desire to include you in my own mission to preserve the world, and to crush the head of Satan. Satan had hoped to crush you, and to submit you to his will. It becomes very humbling for him, then, when you make it clear which side you are on, and you are willing to do your part in this struggle. By yourself, you would not be able to take on Satan; he would be far too strong and too clever for you. That is why I want you to join me, and to become a member of my little army, and you will be protected from the dangers of the evil one. If you want to be close to me, and to feel me close to you, then please become one of my little army, and I will use you for powerful good for the world. No matter what your life circumstances are, no matter how limited your physical or mental capacities are, I can use your goodwill in opposing and overcoming Satan.

I'm sorry for butting in again, but I understood that Satan was al-ready defeated. It seems now as if he was just demoted, but is as deter-mined and as powerful as ever.

Listen to me very carefully now, because it is vital that you understand this clearly, and beyond all doubt. Satan *is* defeated; his fate is sealed, and he will spend all eternity in hell. However, his final and public shame and defeat is being deferred until Jesus has fully established his kingdom. The kingdoms of the world and of Satan will have come to an end, and the kingdom of Jesus Christ will be proclaimed for all eternity. Until then, Satan is not in hell. Four times in the one chapter (Apoc 12) it says 'Satan was cast down to *earth*.' When Jesus came, he called

Satan 'the prince of this world'. Satan brought Jesus to the top of a mountain, and offered him all the kingdoms of the earth, if Jesus would adore him. Oh, yes, this was Satan at his most arrogant. In spite of all that Jesus did, including his death, resurrection, and the coming of the Spirit at Pentecost, Satan is still determined to charge the windmills, and to carry on a war which he cannot win. Pride is enormously destructive, and it is seen at its worst in Satan. There is no way that he could ever accept the fact that he has been defeated. If God offered him forgiveness now, he would turn it down, because to accept forgiveness would mean having to admit that he was wrong, and that is something Satan could never admit. It is for your growth and maturity that Satan is allowed to test you. If you avail of the protection offered to you, then you are never in danger. You have the Spirit of God within you, and he is so much more powerful than any evil spirit you will meet on the road of life. You have me by your side, where I hold your hand, and cast my mantle over you. Like any child, you can choose to let go, and to run out into the traffic, and be severely injured. Satan *is being defeated* just as we speak. The process is on-going. To you is given the wonderful privilege of sharing in that victory. When I ask you to share in the battle, I do so because I want you to share in the victory. You and I know that Satan is defeated, in so far as he can never overcome the good. Sadly, there are those who believe his lies, come under his influence, and are lost to the family of God. Nobody in heaven wants this to happen, but we have to accept the reality of free will, and the responsibility every one bears for the salvation of his/her own soul. Such conquests encourage Satan, and he becomes bolder with each day. Looking around at today's world, you could be excused if you thought that Satan is winning the battle. He certainly gets the front pages of the tabloids, and the peddlers of filth and pornography of all kinds seem to have a thriving market. Once again, I say that the Christian is someone who lives in the knowledge of the victory of Jesus Christ and, at the end of time, everything that challenges or questions that victory will be eternally destroyed.

When people cut themselves off from God, they are in dangerous waters, without paddle or oar. There is a huge number of people today who have dismissed God as a myth. They are cloning babies, and doing their own creating. They are advocating a morality that allows for no barriers or boundaries. They pick and select which babies should be born, and which should die. They have now turned their attention to the elderly, and are applying the same criteria. Because they are playing God, they don't have any need of any other god. It is at this stage that a real problem arises, and I hope that you can understand what I have to say. People are punished *by* their sins, rather than *for* them. Look at the human wreckage of those with wet brains, because of alcohol, with seriously damaged lungs, because of nicotine, or with Aids, because of drugs or irresponsible sex. Human nature seems to contain the seeds of self-destruction. Without the action of the Holy Spirit, it is impossible for human beings to rise above the quicksand of their own selfishness. On their own, people can only sink deeper and deeper into the swamp of death and destruction. This hurts me very much, and I am fully committed to save as many as possible from such a terrible fate. I need *prayer, prayer, prayer*. It matters not what prayers you say, as long as you pray. Naturally, I recommend the Rosary, because Jesus has given this prayer extraordinary graces. It is a prayer that honours me but, because it contains the main events of his life, it also gives him great honour. Michael the Archangel was directly involved in the battle in heaven, and in expelling Satan from there. Therefore, he is still given special powers in the battle against Satan. He should be invoked constantly, and in so doing, my children will be protected against the evil one.

The world is in great peril today. God is anxious to call his children back to him; otherwise he will allow them to be severely punished by their own evil-doing. It is prayer, and prayer alone, that can prevent disaster coming upon us. The horrors of war, and something like the tsunami disaster, is but a shadow of what can befall the world if it does not turn back to God. God *knows* his people. He knows that, in their hearts, they are deaf and blind to their own truth. God never wants to destroy what he has created, but if people continue to ignore him, and his warnings, he will have no choice but to get their attention through severe and awful punishment. It is much better that people should suffer on this earth, if that turns their minds and hearts towards God, than that they should suffer in hell for all eternity. God will do anything to prevent that final disaster. You might take this as if God was *threatening*, and that I am repeating those threats in different parts of the world today. *That is not true*. What I am doing is spelling out very clearly what *will* happen if people do not return to God. In other words, I am speaking about things that can be *avoided* if people make the right decisions. If the disasters happen, then people will clearly see that this is all of their own making. God gives people a choice, and I continue to repeat that choice. Please join me in *prayer*, and all the disasters can be prevented. Prayer is truly powerful. An earthquake could be stopped right in the midst of the action, if enough people joined together in prayer. God threatened the destruction of the town of Ninevah, and Jonah went there and called on the people to repent, so that the threatened destruction would not descend upon them. All of the people, including the king, began to fast and pray, and God relented, and did not inflict the punishment he had threatened. That is the choice that I offer today's world. That is why I ask your help, because I need to involve all of my children in such an enormous undertaking. I want to afford you the privilege of being directly involved in the salvation of the world. I am *calling* on you to join me, because the more that join in this crusade, the sooner the tide of evil and the waves of destruction will be diverted. It breaks my heart to see my children in such danger, and I find consolation from each *individual* who decides to join me, and become one of my loyal army of defenders. I entrust my message to many special souls, and it really saddens me that they have to suffer by being scoffed at, and not taken seriously. It seems that, if people do not like the message, they find an excuse to shoot the messenger. You might as well know that there is a battle to the death between the forces of good and evil in today's world. Jesus said 'They who are not *for* me are *against* me.' There is no 'in-between' anymore. The opposite to love is not hatred, but indifference. It is very difficult to transform indifference, because not only does the person not respond, but has no interest in hearing the message in the first place.

God does not have to be directly involved in many of today's global disasters. As people continue to pollute the atmosphere, that causes a complete climate change. The snow-caps at the Poles begin to melt, and the sea-levels rise. Soon the water levels will be so high that much of the land will be under water. The pressure of the water will evoke eruptions in the seabed, and more and more tidal waves will come rushing in to wipe out whole countries. All of this is of people's making, and so it is only right that they should be held responsible. The greed and selfishness that leads to war, broken families, murders, and genocide is an evil of people's doing. I know Satan is behind it, but it would be too simplistic to blame him for everything. There are people who do not need Satan to tempt them, or to lead them astray. The whole purpose of their lives is self-centred, and the victims of such are always the innocent ones. The blood of the innocent cries out to God for justice. At the beginning of creation, God introduced a plan of great love. When people turned away from God, he introduced a time of great mercy. You are living in that time now. If people do not respond to this, God will introduce a time of infinite justice. I mentioned the Rosary as a powerful prayer at a time like this. I also strongly recommend the Divine Mercy Chaplet, which has people offering 'the Body and Blood of Our Lord Jesus Christ in atonement for our sins, and the sins of the whole world'. As you pray the Chaplet, just imagine that you are standing with me at the foot of the cross. I call on all of my children to rally around me in a crusade of prayer that will change the direction of the world. Only prayer can save the world at this time.

So, as I understand it, we, the people, are being called to undo the damage we have done, and to become actively involved with you, under God, in rescuing the world from self-destruction?

Exactly! With all my heart I call upon my children at this time. It does not have to be a time of gloom, doom, and damnation. *You* can prevent that happening, and I am depending on you to do so. Whatever your call is in life, no matter how great your responsibilities are, I am placing on your shoulders now the greatest responsibility that you will ever have in life. There are *two* parts to this emergency rescue plan. The first is *your prayers*, and the second is *the direct intervention of God*. One will not come without the other. I'm sure you must agree that God cannot be expected to intervene if he is not asked. God acts out of total respect for our free will, and he waits for our willingness and co-operation, before he intervenes in our lives. There is one thing that must be stressed. I am realistic enough to know that *all* of God's people are not prepared to turn to him. I would like to tell you the story of Abraham begging God to spare the cities of Sodom and Gomorrah. This may take some time, but I believe it is worth hearing. 'Abraham approached God and said "Will you destroy both innocent and guilty alike? Suppose you find fifty innocent people there within the city – will you still destroy it, and not spare it for their sakes? Surely you wouldn't do such a thing, destroying the innocent with the guilty?" And the Lord replied "If I find fifty innocent people in Sodom, I will spare the entire city for their sake." Abraham spoke again. "Since I have begun, let me go on and speak further to my Lord, even though I am but dust and ashes. Suppose there are only forty-five? Will you destroy the city for lack of five?" And the Lord said "I will not destroy it if I find forty-five." Then Abraham pressed his request further. "Suppose there are only forty?" And the Lord replied "I will not destroy it if I find forty." "Please don't be angry with me, my Lord", Abraham pleaded. "Let me speak. Suppose only thirty are found?" And the Lord replied "I will not destroy it if I find thirty." Then Abraham said "Since I have dared to speak to the Lord, let me continue – suppose there are only twenty?" And the Lord said "Then I will not destroy it for the sake of the twenty." Finally, Abraham said "Lord, please do not get angry. I will speak but once more. Suppose only ten are found there?" And the Lord said "For the sake of ten, I will not destroy it." (Gen 18) As you know both Sodom and Gomorrah were totally destroyed. You must surely be amazed at the patience of the Lord! *It is people like Abraham that I need today.* I need people who are really prepared to stand between God and his people, and to intercede for them. The prayers of such people have the power to change the history of the world. There is one thing you must remember. I am not asking *you* to change the world. All I am asking you to do is to *pray*, and God will change the world. God has entrusted this power to you, and *he* has put the fate of the world in your hands. Of course, you cannot do this on your own! What I have in mind here is something twofold. Once *you* have committed yourself to pray, you will then recruit others to join you, either separately, or in a group, so that the praying voices increase with each day. Where possible, I advise small groups, but this is not essential. I believe, however, that if you and your friends take on this mission, you will need to meet to sustain and encourage each other, and to strengthen your appeal to new members.

I certainly am willing to take on this task, and it is a wonderful privilege to be able to help you. What worries me, though, is how is your call being answered around the world? I mean I wouldn't like to think that the welfare of the world was depending on the prayers of myself and my friends!

Thanks for the smile! My number one 'recruit' is none other than the Holy Father. Like his wonderful predecessor, Pope John Paul II, who worked tirelessly until his final breath, the present Holy Father prays for the world, and he speaks about the world. Pope John Paul II, despite physical weakness and pain, traversed the globe, welcoming every opportunity to call people back to God. He was a beacon of light in a world of much darkness. By the way, please keep the present Pope especially in your prayers, as he has a heavy burden to carry at this present time. Thankfully I have many wonderful and good people who are responding to my call. There are members of my 'little army' in every country in the world. Were it not for them, the world would be at melt-down stage by now. Each and every individual is unique as is the contribution by each one. The good that comes from your prayers is uniquely the result of your prayers. In other words, if you had not prayed, that good would not have happened. I'm not asking *you* to save the *whole* world. I'm asking for your contribution towards some special grace that is needed somewhere in the world. Imagine the joy that awaits you in heaven, when you discover just how *real* your contribution has been. There is nobody in heaven who has not contributed enormously to the welfare of the world.

Now, to summarise what I have been putting before you here today. This is only our seventh session together, and I have even surprised myself by moving onto this subject so early on. That shows you just how important it is to me. You are my friend and, as my friend, I want you to share my interests. I am *asking* for help here. *I thank you* for responding to my call. Oh, if you only knew how much I love you for what you do for me. If you continue doing as I ask you today, you will never have to ask me for anything for the rest of your life. I will repay you a thousand-fold, and your graces will be many. This is yet another great benefit of your prayers for the world. Please share this session with your praying soul-mates, so they may be encouraged in their endeavours, and have a deeper appreciation of the importance of what they do. Love them for me, and always remember that I say what Jesus says, 'Where two or more of you are gathered in my name, there I am in the midst of you.' I bless you and I thank you for your interest and attention today.

CHAPTER EIGHT

The Rosary

I have referred to the Rosary a few times already, and now I would like to get your full attention for this session, while I share with you just how important it is, and why it is important. The idea of repeating prayers, and using beads, is something that's around for a very long time. If you were at the Wailing Wall of Jerusalem you would hear the Jews around you repeating the same words again and again. If you have ever seen a Muslim sitting on a park bench (or, alas, looking out through the bars of a prison cell), you will notice that they constantly finger their beads as they pray. In this, the Rosary of which I speak is part of the same tradition. There is no need to go into the history of the Rosary, but suffice it to say that it emerged as a prayer several hundreds of years ago. Right from the start, it was considered to be a *powerful* prayer, and a battle (Lepanto) is said to have been won through the people praying the Rosary. St Dominic was a powerful promoter of the Rosary, and he founded an Order of Preachers, whose main source of blessing on their preaching was their fidelity to the Rosary.

If I may come in here, even though you probably will deal with it, but to those who don't understand, it would appear that you are promoting yourself *in this way. I know that is not true, but how can you ask people to spend so much time praying to* you, *rather than going straight to God?*

Yes, of course, I was going to deal with that, so I will deal with it now. Firstly, in heaven, God, his angels, and his saints are totally single-minded, and of one accord when it comes to you. Pray to anyone you want in heaven, and you are very pleasing to God. Take, for example, your Novena of Hope (St Gabriel, Passionist), or your Novena of Grace (St Francis Xavier). When you pray one of these Novenas are you boosting Francis Xavier, or are you giving glory to God? What do you think St Francis will do with the prayers you offer to him? In my case, things are slightly different. Jesus has chosen to honour me in some extraordinary ways. I am still the recipient of infinite blessings resulting from my *Yes* of the Annunciation. That's just the way God is. When you get to heaven, and experience how he showers you with endless blessings because of your *Yes* to him during your life, you will have some idea of what I mean. Jesus has chosen to use me as a two-way conduit between him and his children. Any prayers addressed to me are taken as if addressed to him. He is still my Son; I am still his Mother. It gives Jesus great joy when any of my other children (*you!*) give me some of the honour he gives me. This unites them even closer to him and to me. On the other hand, he loves to pour out his blessings on his children *through* me. From a heavenly perspective, I was seen as central to the whole story of salvation, because the outcome depended totally on my willingness to make myself available, so that God's plan could be put into action. I didn't realise this at the time, but I can see it very clearly now. When you pray to me, your prayers are received by me, with great gratitude, and then they are passed on to God, whether as Father, Son, or Spirit. (Naturally, a prayer to One is a prayer to all *Three*.) That is why I want you to pray to me, because it is really pleasing to God. There was a little hint in your question that I might be trying to give a little boost to my ego. No, I'm joking; I know you didn't mean that. I will be completely upfront with you, and tell you once again that prayers addressed to me give great pleasure to God. I continue to love and serve God, and the prayers of my children are part of that service.

The reason I choose the Rosary as a very powerful and special prayer is that Jesus gets the centre spot. As you recite the prayers, you are reflecting on incidents in the life of Jesus. The

Annunciation is about a Saviour coming. Elizabeth became ec-static because I brought Jesus to her. The shepherds and Wise Men came to Bethlehem to see Jesus, not me. The Assumption and my Crowning in heaven is the final evidence that my faith in the promises of Jesus were fulfilled totally. The first part of the Hail Mary is taken directly from the gospels, as it combines the words of the Archangel Gabriel and Elizabeth. In the second part of the prayer, you ask me to 'pray for us sinners now, and at the hour of our death.' Do you believe that I *listen* to this prayer, and that I *will* answer it? This is a very simple prayer, but it is one that gets my full attention. I guarantee you my full attention, and my willingness to answer this prayer. The main problem is that you can 'rattle off' the prayer, without much attention. This is always the danger with all prayers that are recited by rote. I ask you, *please*, to slow down, and to think of what you are say-ing. If you are praying the Rosary on your own, I ask you to say the words *as slowly as possible*. Better one Hail Mary said with at-tention and devotion that a whole Rosary that is just 'rattled off', the only emphasis being on getting to the fifth decade. When you pray with others, it may not be so easy, and they may 'race through' the prayers, and you have a problem as to whether this is a *prayer*, or just running through the prayer, like a machine that pumps out a string of products in quick succession. You may be in a position to draw their attention to what disturbs you (without being 'preachy'), or you may avail of your opportunity to lead in a decade, and show, through example, how the prayer should be said.

I have often heard it said that the Rosary is 'boring', just continu-ous repetition of the same prayer. How would you respond to that?

When I spoke about Contemplation in an earlier session on prayer, I spoke about reciting a mantra – repeating the same word over and over again. It's not the *word* that matters; it's the sincerity of the heart that desires to pray, and to be detached from whatever words are used. Imagine a young mother with her new baby. She whispers the same words again and again, day after day. She never worries about repeating herself. We are speaking of a *relationship* here, and words are not at the centre of a relationship. In fact, a relationship could be so much off the track that all the words are meaningless and lies. When you pray the prayers of the Rosary, which are addressed to the Father, to the Trinity, and to me, all you have to do is try to ensure that you mean what you say, and know that what you say is very meaningful to us. Anything can become boring that does not have your attention. The Rosary is your gift to me, and I would like to think that, when you give someone a gift, you are very conscious about what you're doing; and, of course, you would be highly offended if the recipient paid absolutely no attention to you, or to the gift that you offer. When you begin to pray the Rosary (notice I avoid the word 'say') just concentrate on what you are doing, and the words you are praying. This is something that you have to *practise* and, in no time at all, you will find yourself praying with real purpose.

Another difficulty that many people experience is how to combine the vocal prayers with the reflections on the various gospel scenes connected with each mystery. Once again, this becomes easy with practice. You imagine the scene, you put yourself into the scene, and you pray quietly, as if you were contemplating a painting on the wall. It is never a question of 100% attention to *both*, as that would be impossible. As you recite the prayers, you are conscious of a particular scene, and this should not distract from the words that you say. If you have a card or a booklet which contains pictures of the mysteries, all the better. Anything that helps you pray with greater attention and devotion is highly recommended. The Rosary has its roots in the gospels and, when you pray it, you are opening your heart to all the graces that flow from what Jesus has done for you. There are very special graces attached to the Rosary. Indeed, I must say they are truly unique. If people understood the *power* of the Rosary, they would never leave the beads out of their hands. It is such a simple, uncomplicated prayer, that it may be difficult to appreciate its power and importance. *The Rosary is Jesus' gift to you*. It is his way of honouring me, and he gets great delight in it.

Nothing remains the same, as all God's people, and all of God's creation, continue to evolve and develop. That is why I do not condemn television, and all the other many distractions that seem to have stifled the Rosary as a family prayer. I honestly believe that, if people *wanted* to pray, the presence of a television set would not deter them. Of course, it can be a distraction but, for those who are not sincerely committed to prayer, there is never a shortage of distractions. If there isn't one, they create one! Oh how I wish I could have the custom of the family Rosary restored. It provides such sure and certain protection to the home and family, and is a source of much blessings to others. I can *ask* people to do this, and I can pray that it happens. It is getting more difficult to be heard amidst the clamour of television, radio, and all the electrical and mechanical gadgets which people surround themselves with today. I have no choice but to ask and to pray, and to trust my friends, such as you, to do what you can to convey this message to others. You may not have much success. That's not what matters. All you are asked to do is to try, and leave the responsibility for the reply to those to whom you speak. In Lourdes, Fatima, Medjugorje, etc., I have personally appealed for the family Rosary to be restored. I have had a good response from many, and complete indifference from many others. What bothers me is that many people who call themselves Christian can be completely indifferent to my personal pleas. There are millions in the world who know nothing about Jesus or myself, and they will not be held responsible. Surely it is only right that those who claim to accept the gospel, and to be influenced by it, should give special attention to what I say when I appear among them. Living in an electronic world, they might consider devising a gadget that would recite the Rosary for them! Those who spend long hours looking at a television set, or a computer screen, will soon find that they have little time left for anything else. After all, you and I know that praying the Rosary is simply a question of finding the *time*, and of freely giving that time to me. If you are too busy to pray a Rosary, then you are too busy. I'm sure you'll admit that you will always 'find' time, if there is something interesting on television, or there is a show that you want to see. It is very sad, indeed, that something as precious and as powerful as the Rosary should receive total indifference and disinterest.

Satan hates the Rosary, because it is a whip that beats him into submission. He will never accept that such a simple prayer can have such extraordinary power. In our last session, I spoke about praying for the world in which you live. The Rosary is an ideal prayer for such an intention. Jesus has decreed it this way, and I am grateful and delighted that he has. Those who make the Rosary an important part of their prayer-life are a powerful defence against the evil one. After the Eucharist itself, the Rosary is the most powerful prayer. You can recite it anywhere or anytime. You do not require others to be with you, even though it is such a wonderful blessing to be able to recite the Rosary with others. If you are a 'keep-fit' person, you can walk the country roads, or the beach, and pray the Rosary all the way. What a time of great blessing for both body and soul. You have a choice of using a Rosary ring instead of a beads, if you wish to pray as you walk in public.

From my own limited experience, I know I have favourite prayers, and there are some that come easier to me than others. I gather from you, that, even if I find it difficult, the Rosary is a prayer that I should never shy away from, no matter how difficult I find it.

Oh, well said! Please, I beg you, listen to what I tell you now. If you accept within your heart that the Rosary is truly powerful, and is a prayer that gives me great joy and consolation, then you will resolve to approach it from a completely different angle. I want you to take it on as a mission; as part of a contract with me. I will pour so many blessings on you that you will welcome each and every opportunity to recite it. I can give you the grace to *love* the Rosary. Before I can do that, however, you must be willing to take on this service to me for the sake of others. I want you to think seriously about this commitment, because it is a very serious commitment. This applies to all prayer, of course. If you are willing to develop a prayerful heart, I will ask the Spirit to give you that, and I myself will come and live in your heart. I am prepared to pray with you, for you, and in you. What a joy it would give me to instil a love of the Rosary in your heart. You mentioned earlier about the Rosary been boring, and now you refer to it as a difficult prayer. I know you are just asking a question, and these points do not apply to you. However, I take this opportunity to express a certain degree of disappointment that many people never seem to have been instructed properly in the recitation of the Rosary. The youngest child can recite it, if it is properly and simply presented. Reciting the same prayer again and again, is part of the prayers of all the great world religions. Remember it is not the *words* that make it a prayer, but the attitude of heart of the one who is praying. If you lead with your tongue, and your heart doesn't follow, you will very soon get tired, bored, and discouraged. Stay downstairs in your heart, and let your heart lead you. Imagine you have a slide projector down there that is showing various scenes from each of the mysteries. You just watch the picture, and whisper your prayer. I *love* to hear that prayer, and can never tire listening to it. There are no prayer books in heaven. There are no Rosary beads there either. All the angels and saints do is sing the praises of God, day and night. 'Glory! Holy Holy! Praise and Thanks be to our God!' The same words will go on for all eternity – and I promise you that you won't get bored, nor will you find it difficult. It would be no harm, indeed, if on occasions you imagined you were standing before me in heaven and praying the Rosary to me. You could also make sure that you include me in each of the mysteries, and you can speak to me there. Anything that will make the Rosary come alive is very good.

Thankfully, my special son, Pope John Paul II, added the Mysteries of Light to what was there before. (I'll let you in on a secret! It was I who suggested to him that he should do this. He was such a wonderful example to all of you, and he was a great joy to my heart, and continues to be so, now that he is with me in heaven.) Even with these extra mysteries, you don't have to confine yourself to them. You can sit with me in our little back garden in Nazareth, or you can join with me as I wait for Easter. You can travel with me as I take up the rear behind Jesus and his followers, as he walked the roads of Galilee. There is no end to choices for those who are *willing* to take on this prayer with a generous heart, and a prayerful spirit. *Willingness* is the key that opens all human hearts. If you have this, I will do everything else. I get great excitement in my heart when the opportunity arises to reveal to one of my children just how wonderful, and yet how simple, this prayer really is. I never miss an opportunity, because I rejoice when any of my children step forth to share in the treasures of heaven. Just turn to me, and with all the willingness you can muster, tell me that you wish to make this prayer the strongest bond between us. I promise that I will never let go of my side of that bond. I use the word 'bond' very deliberately, because the bond between mother and child is life-giving, and life-sustaining. Oh, my heart is so filled with joy as I speak to you now. I also rejoice in the fact that this message will be placed in the hands of many others, and I will ensure that my words reach their hearts.

The shortest way to come to love and appreciate the Rosary is to *recite* it, rather than debate or discuss it. You learned to walk by walking, and you learned to talk by talking. This is how you will familiarise yourself with the Rosary, and develop a great and special love for it. When you travel a road for the first time, it can appear to be quite long. The oftener you travel it, the shorter it seems to get. It is the same with the Rosary except that, as you come to love it more and more, you will want to give more time to the slow and reverent recitation of the prayers, so your time with me will get longer. If you are not already someone for whom the Rosary is at the centre of your prayer-life, then you might like to begin by praying just one decade, and returning to it later on. All I am asking is that you *begin*, and the whole process will follow. I know you would love to discover the secrets of this wonderful prayer, and I am here, willing and ready to teach you all of that. This is a happy and blessed moment for both of us. We have talked about it long enough, and we have spent enough time to have said at least one Rosary. Seriously, this is time well-spent if it helps to deepen your appreciation and understanding of, and your commitment to this prayer.

Now let me summarise what we have talked about today. I spoke of the Rosary in a general way, at the beginning: of its composition, and its significance in the economy of grace and God's blessings. I deliberately held back, and spoke of various aspects, and of various methods, before getting on to what was in my heart to say to you. Right from the beginning, I wanted to come straight out and ask you to *pray the Rosary ... pray the Rosary ... pray the Rosary*. I know that, if you did that, everything else would follow. However, it was important that I should first deal with any questions you had, and to speak about my own hopes for this prayer, and its effect on the history of the world. I ended up where I wanted to start. I ended up asking you to declare your willingness to make this prayer a central plank in your prayer-life; to just go and 'pray it' and leave the rest to me. I spoke of it as establishing a unique Mother and child bond between us – a bond that will last for all eternity. 'Catch' the rhythm of the mantra of the prayers, and your heart will pray along like a song. These sessions we are having together are based on the idea of returning to Playschool with me, so that I can teach you many things that I want you to know. Every time you recite the Rosary, take it that you are back in Playschool, and the learning process becomes endless. Thank you. Thank you. Thank you. I enjoyed our session today!

CHAPTER NINE

Purity

I am very aware that what I want to share with you today may not get a very wide audience. However, it is something that is dear to my heart, and I cannot delay any longer in speaking about it. Purity could be defined in a dictionary as 'pureness, cleanness, freedom from physical or moral pollution'. God created you; you are created in his image and likeness, and you must do all within your power to preserve the purity and integrity of your soul. This is based, primarily, on *truth*. If your heart is open to truth, you will live within the confines of God's expectations of you. That is why the Holy Spirit is called the Spirit of Truth. If this Spirit is given his way to live and to work within you, you will be guided by instincts of pure love, and of honest living. Human nature is extremely weak and, without the power of the Spirit, it can easily succumb to all temptations, and to all attractions, whether good or not. From the very start I want to stress that I will not be speaking just about sex here, though that will be central to most of what I have to say. Sex has a very important role to play in God's plan for his children and, like all of God's gifts, it is *good*. It is the *abuse* of the gift that does the great damage, that spoils God's plans, and that leads people astray, where many of them end up being eternally lost.

Sorry for coming in so early, but I am very interested in what you want to say to me today. That is why I want to make sure that I understand exactly what you have to say, and what I should believe. There is an accepted belief among many people that sex has been turned into something less than good; that it contains a minefield of dangers, and that it is at the centre of all the sins of the world. Do you think that the

Church (and our parents) have placed an unholy stress on sex, so that its beauty and gift is seldom appreciated?

Yes, I'm sure you have heard that and, no doubt, a lot of what you say is true. That is why I am speaking to you now. Despite anything you have heard or believed in the past, I want to 'tidy up' this whole issue of purity, so that you will know what I believe, and what I see as the truth. You will notice that I use the word 'purity', because I want to stress the positive and the good, rather than condemn the evil. Jesus said he did not come to condemn the world, and it is not my wish to do so either. What bothers me, indeed, troubles me greatly, is how sex seems to be treated so superficially, and the moral boundaries are being eroded all the time. If God wanted a permissive society, he would have given you Ten Suggestions instead of Ten Commandments! A sin is a sin is a sin. Purity is something that applies to all of God's people, and it makes no distinction between the married or unmarried. The ones who are married have equal responsibility for chastity as have those who are celibate. I am not at all talking here about a husband and wife expressing their love in a sexual way, providing, of course, that the act is sincere and there is mutual fidelity to each other. If one party is being unfaithful, then this expression of love is totally false, and is a lie. When it is open, honest, responsible, and mutually expressed, it becomes one of the most beautiful gifts that God has given his children. My *real* problem is that anything less than that is *damaging* by its very nature. Many a pillow is wet with tears from those who have been used, abused, or irresponsible in their sexual expressions. I am not saying it is always easy to remain faithful, but for a person who lives by the truth, and who wants to preserve his/her own personal integrity, there is no choice. There is extraordinary joy and happiness for those who live lives of purity, and who are faithful to a spouse, to their conscience and, therefore, to God. Only those who travel this road can possibly appreciate what I am saying. Any other road is fraught with heart-break, disruption, and pain. There is no point in pretending otherwise.

When I speak about purity, I am speaking of purity of mind and body. It's not a question of innocence being the absence of opportunity. Lust is the opposite to purity, and it could be defined as 'animal desire for sexual indulgence'. It is one of what are called The Seven Deadly Sins, which summarise human nature's basic weaknesses. The sex drive is an appetite, just as you have an appetite for food or drink. An appetite is a desire to satisfy natural necessities. Lust is the sexual appetite run riot. When an appetite runs riot, it leads to enormous damage, as you know from alcoholism, and obesity. The 'powers that be' seem to be more concerned about the abuse of food and drink than the abuse of sex. With the growing menace of Aids spreading across the globe, the 'scientific' solution is the supply of condoms. Certain groups who have advocated abstinence from sex have been laughed to scorn. Many people seem to have lost their way in what is now called the 'sexual revolution'. This is a reaction to what was seen as the strict Victorian norms of previous generations. Unfortunately, many in previous generations were no better than many are today but, without television and the tabloids, people were not aware of this. However, no matter what people advocate, or no matter how the tabloids glamorise sex, God still holds you accountable for your actions. Purity is an ideal, and an ideal is a vision of the practical. It is completely wrong to think of God as a 'spoil-sport', always raining on your party, and setting boundaries that are difficult to observe. This is completely wrong. God has but one interest, and that is *your good*. Sexual deviance has wrecked ferocious havoc among so many of God's children. I said in an earlier session that you are punished *by* your sins, rather than *for* them. Nowhere is that more evident than in the whole area of sex. The scourge of Aids is one very clear and public result of promiscuity, or irresponsible sex. The wreckage in relationships, because of sex divorced from truth and purity, is also very destructive, and many such people end up on drugs, medication, or suicide. Many of today's murders are a direct result of unrestrained lust. Yes, of course, of its very nature, lust is destructive.

What role do you play in protecting people from themselves, and in preserving purity as a virtue among people?

I am very directly involved in this, because the exploitation and abuse of sex is something that greatly concerns me. Purity is a *virtue*, which is moral excellence, uprightness, or goodness. This is something that is very close to my heart. In former generations, what was called 'The Three Hail Marys' was part of most people's morning and night prayers. Each Hail Mary was followed by the prayer 'Oh, Mary, by Thy pure and Immaculate Conception, make my body pure and my soul holy.' If the mind is not pure, the body cannot be. 'My strength is as the strength of ten, because my heart is pure.' 'A pure heart create in me, and put a steadfast spirit within me' was the prayer of the Psalmist. All lust comes from within, as Jesus said. What is bred in the spirit will come out in the actions. That is why an uncontrolled desire or fantasy can become sinful, even if not put into action. The root of the evil is nurtured, and it is only a short step to the action. I am not saying that *thoughts* or *feelings* are sinful. Feelings, of themselves, have no morality. They are neither right nor wrong. However, if you nourish them, and entertain them, you run the risk of acting on them. Purity of heart prevents all wrong thinking, unhealthy fantasies, and lustful desires from gaining a foothold within your spirit, and the evil is prevented before it comes forth in action. *It is not possible to have a pure heart without prayer.* This is where I come in. I am most anxious to preserve the virtue of purity within the hearts of all my children. It is normal for parents to do what they can to prevent their children from damaging themselves through irresponsible sex. Sometimes a fear of intrusion, or a sense of inadequacy prevents them being positive, definite, and uncompromising in the advice they give their children. I could never be accused of that. Those responsible have a serious obligation to ensure that the children have a sound grounding in clear and unambiguous sex education. Many of the children grow up in families, attend school, and attend church, and they never get one straight forthright talk on sex. What are adults afraid of? Are they uncomfortable with their own sexual experiences, and feel totally inadequate to speak with authority? Many of these adults will attend night classes for every subject under the sun, but they don't know where to turn for help in carrying out one of their most serious and far-reaching responsibilities. I'm sorry, because I have wandered off from answering the question you asked. Yes, indeed, I am there, with all the help that is needed, for any child of mine to live a pure and sinless life. In fact, if you are a child of mine, I expect you to lay great store on the virtue of purity.

Remember I am placing before you the *ideal*, knowing that you may not always succeed in attaining it. When Jesus rescued the woman taken in adultery, who was going to be stoned to death, he asked her 'Has anyone condemned you?' 'No' was her reply. 'Then neither do I condemn you. Go in peace *and sin no more.*' He did not condemn her, but he did not say that what she did was alright. I say the same to any of my children who have failed to live up to the ideal along the way. I do not condemn you; go in peace, and take every precaution that it does not happen again. You are not an angel, a disembodied spirit, and it is only normal and natural that your sexuality should makes demands on you, just as a recovering alcoholic can experience a very strong desire for a drink. Just as the alcoholic, if he wants to preserve his sobriety, must not give in to the temptation, so must you oppose any unreal demands your sexuality may make on you. From experience, you will know that this stance will result in peace, and in a sense of well-being. Whole lives have been ruined by a lust that was allowed run riot for a very short period of time. When the lust is satisfied, it can be followed by a deep personal sense of self-disgust, and of guilt. 'By their fruits you shall know them.' That experience was not from God.

And now I want to come to the most serious dimension of this battle to preserve your purity of mind and body. *It is Satan's greatest weapon in his attack upon my children.* Any evil that attaches to lust is the result of its source, the evil one himself. Satan knows that he has a powerful weapon at his disposal in the sex drive, which God had included in his creation as a *good*. Satan has so many resources at his disposal. It is almost impossible to watch a television programme, read a magazine or a newspaper, without being bombarded with sex that is completely divorced from love. An advertisement for a car is enhanced by a half-naked female draped across the bonnet. As a *woman*, I weep to see how women are exploited in so many ways, and it is sadder still that many of these women allow this to happen for the money it earns them. The extremes of horror include white slavery, where women from impoverished backgrounds are sold as sex slaves. This is a sin that cries to heaven for justice, and it will be punished, and punished severely. No human being of any religion, or none, can possibly excuse such a practice, and they *know* it is wrong. Their ill-gotten wealth will bring them neither peace nor happiness. And then there are the prostitutes, who are just tools in the hands of unscrupulous pimps, and who have been deprived of all human dignity, and any hope of a worthwhile independent and respectable existence. The tidal wave of child abuse that has been revealed over the past few years, and that continues even today, is something that causes great outrage in heaven. Yes, unfortunately, human nature is capable of sinking to extraordinary levels. The *one* person who rejoices in all of this is Satan. Oh, I beg you, my child, please help me to rob him of all the victories of which he boasts. You begin with yourself and, through prayer, you gain blessings for many others in their struggles. To take a clear and definite stand on *purity* is something that infuriates Satan. This is an area that he thought he had claimed to himself, but he cannot be allowed do this to my children. What I am saying in this session may not be welcomed by everybody but, please believe me, *it must be said*. The kingdom of Satan and the kingdom of this world are happy bedfellows. It is as if Satan and the world have made a joint contract to flood the world with pornography, and to provide sex as an industry, instead of a special gift from God. The main reason for this, of course, is *greed*, because there is huge money to be made out of this. Greed knows of no moral boundaries, and love, respect, and dignity do not figure in its vocabulary.

I'm sure you can identify Satan in the work of corrupting morals, and breaking down the fabric of family-life.

Yes, indeed, Satan is waging a full-scale war against the family. I could hardly blame you if you began to think that Satan is winning this one. His trump card is because the sex drive is part of every human being, so he does not have to import or implant anything from outside. All he has to do is to titillate, and to display his false and empty promises in every possible form, and many become mesmerised, and fall for the lie. Please be certain that it is a *lie*, which is the hallmark of Satan. The greatest tragedy of irresponsible sex is that so many pregnancies end up in abortion. This is the slaughter of the innocents all over again. A young vulnerable and panicked teenager can run for an abortion, thinking that that will solve her problem. Imagine her shock to discover her real pain begins *after* the abortion. It is often easier to make a decision, than to have to live with the consequences of that decision. There is no earthly joy that can equate the peace and sense of dignity and worth that resides within the hearts of those who practise purity of mind and body. This brings a much greater joy than anything Satan has to offer. Unfortunately, people are frail, and many will settle for the immediate. Instead of being guided by moral values, or by the commandments of God, they live with a 'situation ethic' attitude, which means they can alter, or make up the rules as they go along, and as it suits them. Once they can justify it, it becomes alright. They have no such things as universal norms. *Lust is always wrong.* When God instructed Adam and Eve in the Garden, he was *serious*, as they found out to their cost. It is obvious that the tide of promiscuity is being severely punished in today's world. Some of the harm is fatal (Aids), some is wrecking great damage to the body (VD, etc), and most is unseen, but can be heard through the sobs on the pillow at night. Broken homes, wrecked marriages, and transient relationships that include children, can be very damaging to those children. It is not always possible (or wise) for a couple to 'stay together' in a marriage. There are times when it is better for all concerned that the parents separate. I am not blaming anyone for this, even if it is often caused by the selfishness of one or both. Human relationships can be very frail and fragile. A relationship that is not moving forward is, automatically, moving backwards. A relationship that is not worked on will end up in shipwreck. The greatest gift a father can give his children is that he should love their mother. If this happens, both parents and children will be protected from much unnecessary hurt.

How do you see the situation of young people today, growing up in a culture that glorifies sex, and that trivialises everything their parents held as sacred? It must be really difficult for such youth to take purity on board as an ideal to strive for.

Firstly, despite everything, I believe that the youth of today are as good as any generation that ever went before. Everything is changing around them, but it is important to remember that, as the world around changes, so do the people who live in it. The youth of today have a strength and a resilience that their grandparents did not have, or need. I am not saying that they all use that strength, but they certainly have it. They are well informed. They know about the advance of Aids and other sexually-transmitted diseases. They witness many families breaking up, they witness young girls getting pregnant, and being abandoned by a man who spoke words of undying love some months previously. It is unrealistic to expect the same level of maturity from all young people. Some are mature beyond their years, and others just never grow up. This latter group live in a world that is peopled by objects called people, which are there to be used like everything else that comes to hand. As well as destroying the lives of others, they are dead-bent on the road of self-destruction. They know it all, and you can't tell them anything. My heart goes out to them in a special way, because they are so vulnerable. It is only through God's power that they can be guided through the minefield of adolescence. I would sincerely ask you to join me in praying for such as these. You may feel helpless in stemming the tide of pornography that is coming at people. The fact is that you are powerless, but not helpless, and certainly not hopeless. *Satan cannot overcome good, even if he is seen to be successful for a time.* Do not lose hope, and I will provide you with many opportunities to share what I am sharing with you today. You have a responsibility to do so, because your silence would be serious moral cowardice, and you would betray me. I am not asking you to stand at the street corner and start preaching. All I am asking you is that, *when the opportunity arises*, with a member of your family, or over a cup of tea with a friend, you share your concern. By doing this, you may evoke the concern of another, and so the good begins to spread. It would be a tragedy if you allowed yourself to think that the task is impossible, and there is no point in trying to stop the in-coming tide with a spoon. *You do matter*, and for everyone who joins forces with me in promoting purity, and upholding moral values, there is formed a solid and sturdy wall against the onslaughts of Satan.

I need to conclude. I hope today's session was not too 'heavy' for you. It is something, however, that concerns me greatly, and I just had to introduce it now. Don't forget, I am not talking about, or looking for, perfection here. You are not saints. All you can do is do your best, even if you fail on occasions. Purity is about *attitude* rather than about *actions*. If the compass of your life is pointed towards *purity* as something you want to cultivate and sustain, then the Spirit will ensure that that this is exactly what will happen. I regret that I seldom used the word *love* in this session, because that is what it is all about. God is love, and they who live in love, live in God, and God lives in them. If you share in the love of God, you will have more than enough love to love others, without seeking to meet your own needs, or to use others for your own gratification. If you know what love is, you will demand and expect that from another, before you make a contract to spend your life with that person. This may not make you the 'belle of the ball', but you will have earned respect, while preserving your own integrity. If you fail or fall along this path, I will be only too willing to help you, and to enable you walk with dignity again. To err is human, to forgive is divine. No matter how many times you fail, *never lose sight of the ideal.* God respects you so much that he expects the best from you. Sometimes your best may not be enough, and God has no problem understanding that. The compass of your life keeps pointing towards the good and, if it does, then, you can be sure that you will reach that good. Thank you for listening to me today. I feel that I have shared something very special with you and that, of course, confirms the truth that you are very special.

CHAPTER TEN

Family

I spoke in our last session about my pain over Satan's attacks on families, and on family life today. I grew up in a very special family, and I had the privilege of being the wife and the mother in the most important family that ever lived on this earth. You can imagine just how important family is to me. I am a Mother, and I always will be. You are part of my family, and you have many brothers and sisters within the family of God that are all equally dear to me. I can identify very easily with parents, and they are never out of my thoughts and concerns. When you were born, you were born into a particular family. You inherited a name and a home and perhaps some brothers and sisters. Very shortly after your birth, you were brought to church for baptism, and there you were enrolled and adopted into the family of God. At that moment, I became your heavenly Mother. You were too young to appreciate what was going on, but I certainly took that occasion very seriously. When a child is adopted into a family, that child inherits parents, a home and perhaps brothers and sisters. Supposing it is you who was adopted. You now know that that family is *real*, and *you* helped make it complete. The adoption was so much more than just a ritual or a ceremony. You *really* became a member of that family. What I am looking for now is that you would adopt *me* into your family, so that I would become a *real* member of your family. This is something that I would greatly treasure and appreciate anyhow, but, because of the concern I expressed about the attacks on the family, it is just a great joy for me to be a member of your family. Satan would not dare touch a family, of which I am a member.

Of course I would really love that, but you will have to let me know exactly what I should do to ensure that that happens.

From your point of view that will be easy enough. All I ask is a willingness to accept me, and to acknowledge me. For example, you don't welcome visitors into your home by opening the door, letting them in, and then ignoring them. I'm sure you have known or heard of families where hospitality is so special that the visitor is made to feel at home straight away. The visitor is made to feel as one of the family. I want to become one of your family, and I want to be totally integrated into that family. A picture or a statue can help, because all such things help to remind. However, my presence has to be more than that. There are other pictures in your house, some of relatives in distant places, and several of relatives who are dead. Naturally, I require more than that. If I am to protect the family from the assaults of Satan, then I have to become a *real living* member, who is acknowledged by all, and who is constantly involved in all that happens within the family. You can begin, of course, by displaying pictures or statues (not too many!). The next stage is to *consecrate* your home to my Immaculate Heart. Be willing to accept me with the particular expertise I bring to a family as a Mother. You then 'gather around' me (not physically), and make me the centre of your home. The picture or the statue can become your Prayer Place, as you gather around me to pray. The more you defer to my presence, the more aware you become of my presence, the stronger my influence can be. Please remember that I am speaking of a *definite* presence here. I want to be *really* present among you, and to be accepted and acknowledged as being there. In most homes the mother never runs short of things to do. There are so many things to take care of in a home, especially when there are dependents, either young or old. I am a very *active* Mother, and I am always on the look-out for people and situations that require attention.

Is it possible for such a family to become aware *of your presence and of your protection? How would you say that your presence effects the atmosphere in the house?*

I can assure you that my presence will become quite evident to those who want to see. If you do not advert to my presence, of course, then you are treating me like a 'posh' visitor that is confined to the front parlour, and never allowed into those parts of the house where the real life is lived. You can actually acknowledge my presence in such a way that you, and everyone in the house, *know* that the home is entrusted to my care. You pray to me, not as someone who is away in heaven somewhere, but as someone who is right there with you. According as you make my presence more real, so will my presence become more evident. It is good to have a picture or a statue near the entrance, so that it is the first thing that catches the eye upon entering, and the last thing to see upon leaving. There is no need to overdo the pictures and statue bit! I will know, and you will know when I have been fully accepted as the Mother and protector of your home. Be sensitive in your choice of pictures or statues. In a family of young children, icons may not have any great meaning. There are pictures and statues that represent me as I appeared at Lourdes, Fatima, Medjugorje. There are other images that have been painted under the direction of some special soul who is chosen to act as my spokesperson to others. Ensure that your picture or statue is 'relevant' and attractive, so that they get as much attention as possible. A picture or statue is a 'sacramental', which is a sacred object that protects from the evil one the people and places where it is displayed. It is my ardent desire to be as consciously present to the family members as they are to each other. I depend on them to allow this take place. After all, I am not coming into your home for a holiday. I am coming to be constantly on the watch, and to protect this home, and everyone in it, from everything that might harm them in any way. You asked if my presence would effect the atmosphere in the home. If I may say so, I am much more than just a purifier that recycles the air, refreshes it, and purifies it. The atmosphere in a home is very important. You cannot renew people, nor can you corrupt them. You renew the atmosphere in which they live, and they become renewed, or you corrupt the atmosphere in which they work, and they become corrupted. The young child may never hear a cross word between Mammy and Daddy, but if there is tension between them, Junior will begin to bite his nails, wet the bed, etc. The atmosphere will get to him, no matter how careful the parents are to protect him from what is going on in the background. That is why I consider my presence in a home as a guarantee to preserve the purity and the peace of the atmosphere. There is no way that Satan can infiltrate a home which is under my protection. When Satan knocks on your door, just call me, and let me answer it!

The prayer-life in such a home should continue to grow in a two-fold way. There should be a definite time each day when my children gather around me for a Rosary and other prayers. If a mother is on her own in the home, we can have a very worthwhile time together. It is important that the mother understands that I am not there to replace her, to undermine her authority, or to give her an excuse for doing nothing. I bless all that she does, and guide her decisions and actions. We share so much in common, and it is just very special when the mother is deeply aware of this reality. Together we can work wonders in this home. Children hold a very special place in my heart, and I watch over them at all times, in their coming and going, and when they are away from the home. The custom of using Holy Water as people leave the home, and return to it, is something I greatly encourage. Wearing a Miraculous Medal, a Matrix Medal, or a scapular, is another way I use as a protection. Such people are wrapped in my mantle, and Satan has no control over them in any way. My protection is as strong and as certain as I am allowed to provide. It gives me great joy to be able to provide this protection, because the family is my prime target of blessing, knowing that it is also the prime target of Satan in his attempts to destroy the good. I stand guard at each door and window of

such homes, and Satan is never allowed entry. If families realised just how *real* my presence and protection is, they would
never neglect to avail of that at all times.

What is it that you believe a family should do to maximise the effect
of your presence among them? How can we best give you a 'free hand'
in carrying out all that you wish to do among the family members, and
within the family home?

There is a process here. Normally a family take out insurance
against theft, fire, or personal injury, and it is right that they
should do so. Not all families are aware of the *real* danger, and
they have no protection against Satan, and his attacks. The first
stage is to become aware of this. Once a parent (enough to start
with) becomes aware of this danger, he/she begins to set up a
plan of protection. This may begin with the display of a picture
and a statue. This *must* be followed by a consecration of the
home to my Immaculate Heart. The family then develop a pat-
tern of prayer with me, which should include a Rosary and, perhaps Novenas and private prayer. And then the *real* miracle
takes place. I no longer remain just a picture on a wall, or a statue
on a pedestal, when I am invited and allowed to enter the heart
of each individual, and become the caretaker there. This is the
process; this is the journey. It would be a tragedy to stop this
process somewhere along the way, before it has been brought to
completion. I do not ask, nor do I expect that every member of
the family should goose-step together, and be totally of one
mind on all of this. Each of my children is unique, and I respect
that difference. What matters is that a parent, who has the responsibility to give leadership, should try to guide the family in
the direction that I have outlined. Just as the parents desire that
each of the children should be personally involved in this
process, so will I ensure that this will happen, in time. It may
take a while, but it will happen. A parent is limited in the influence that he/she can exert on the children, but I will be there to
bless their efforts, and to ensure that they succeed. All I need is

an entry, and once I have entered into the situation, I will begin work straightaway. It will give great encouragement and confidence to the parent when the lead that is given begins to produce results.

Just as the parents are the first and primary teachers of their children, so do I consider the family unit as the core of the parish Christian community. Most parishes are too large to consider one as a community. The parish is a community of communities. Each family is like a separate stream that flows into the same sea. The role of a parent is a difficult and demanding one, but the rewards are enormous. It is sad when parents take this serious responsibility to themselves, and see no need for any Divine assistance. Such parents wish their children to be much better than *they* are, and they end up being disappointed that their children are no better than that. Many serious results follow when insecure parents are rearing more insecure children. There are certain weaknesses, addictions, and aggressive attitudes passed on from one generation to another. This will continue, unless the chain is broken. Many people blame their parents for how they are today; yet they, in turn, can easily pass on all of that unhealthiness to the next generation. I am most anxious to break such a chain, and I can do so, if allowed. There is a big difference between a house and a home. The house is built of bricks and sand, but a home is built on love. Because God is love, wherever I am, I will ensure that love is present. Where there is love, there is God, and surely no family could ask for a greater blessing. The Christian family is an extension of the family of God, and it would be sad if those who consider themselves Christian, should become so involved with the urgent that they completely neglect the important. Some people spend a lot of time and money in tending and nurturing shrubs and flowers in their gardens, and they can take rightful pride in the result, which draws the attention and admiration of passers-by. The most precious 'plant' in a house is a child, and parents should avail of all help, human and Divine, to ensure that their children get the best possible start in life. Once again, I say that the atmosphere within the home is what contributes to healthy and wholesome growth. This is something that I can *guarantee*. This is a *gift* that I offer to any family that wants it. I am always on 'stand-by', waiting for every opportunity to become part of any family that allows me become a member. Their home will become my home and, I can assure you that I will make my home there, and I will be at home, and feel at home among the members of my adopted family.

Consecration implies making something sacred. A home that is consecrated becomes a sacred place. When I lived on this earth, there was awesome reverence for the Holy of Holies in the Temple. It was there that God lived, and no one but the High Priest would dare enter there. When Jesus died on Calvary, the veil of the Temple was torn in two, and the Holy of Holies was thrown open to all who wished to enter. Even to this day, no Jew would dare enter that sacred place. In Jerusalem, the old Temple lies in ruins, and will do so until the end of time. The reason for this is that, somewhere among those ruins, is the Holy of Holies, and no Jew will venture there for fear of walking on the Holy of Holies. The Christian family can make their home a Holy of Holies. It can be a place where God dwells, and where I am en-trusted with its welfare and happiness. There is much talk today about the soaring price of houses, especially in urban areas. A home which contains a Christian family is *priceless*. The angels hover over it and protect it, because I call on them to do so. Visitors coming and going from such a home are sure to be aware of the sense of peace and happiness that prevails there. The hospitality is special, and food that is prepared with love al-ways tastes well. The hallmark of Satan is division and confus-ion. Such is not present in the Christian home, where the mem-bers share the same Spirit, and are confident and secure in their lives. The products of such a home become wonderful influ-ences for good wherever they go in life. The parents are sowing the seeds, and many future generations will reap the harvest. The road to heaven is heaven, just as the road to hell is hell. It is more difficult to get heaven into people than to get people into heaven. Rather than concentrating on getting to heaven, you should be ready to do what you can to get heaven down here. There are people around you who are living in hell, and you can bring heaven to them. A Christian home is like an oasis in a desert, where others come to be nourished and to be revived. Hospitality is always the hallmark of the Christian home, and many such people often entertain Jesus himself, in the disguise of some poor suffering soul. I'm sure you will agree that I would want the home, where I am enthroned as caretaker, to have an open-door policy to all of those whom the Lord sends to the door. My experience in Bethlehem is something that I still remember. Hospitality towards the visitor is a wonderful example for the children, something they will carry into life with them.

I must finish soon, as you probably have enough to go on with. What I speak of today is something that I pray and long for. It is strongly motivated by two important reasons. Firstly, as your Mother, I very definitely want to be accepted and acknowledged as the Mother in a Christian home, so that I can protect and bless my children. Secondly, I am very conscious of the very deliberate and public attacks that Satan is launching against all forms of family structures. It is still my responsibility to crush his head, and there is no better place to do this than at the front door of a Christian home. I am sounding an alert in today's session, while also assuring safety and protection. Satan has no claim on you whatsoever, and he should be confronted at every turn. I will lead you in the counterattack, so that your home will be a place of victory, and a foretaste of the joys of heaven. I thank you for your attention today, and please know that you are under my loving gaze and protection within your home, and in your coming and going.

CHAPTER ELEVEN

The Divine Mercy

I am really excited about what I want to say to you today. It gives me great joy to be a messenger of good news, and what I have to say to you is certainly good news. I have spoken in a previous session about forgiveness, and the great mercy of God, the forgiving Father. Despite the pulpit-thumping of a previous generation, the church still spoke of a forgiving and loving God. In their wildest dreams, however, they could never have believed or accepted what Jesus was going to reveal some years ago now. It was as if he tore up the script, and said 'Look, this is how I want to do things now. I am offering you something entirely new, and it comes without strings or conditions.' (This, of course, is not new, but it is presented in a very new way, compared to what was presented in the past.) That offering is what is called the Devotion to the Divine Mercy. I cannot possibly exaggerate how extraordinary and precious this is. Here is Jesus *offering* complete and total forgiveness to all who accept it. It is as if he came down off the cross, walked straight over to you, embraced you, and whispered 'I'm going back on the cross to complete the sacrifice, because I'm doing this for *you*.' On many occasions it has been my wonderful privilege to speak about the mercy and love of God. On this occasion, however, Jesus came in person to St Faustina, and he told her that he was offering an unconditional truce, or amnesty. All people had to do was come to him, and allow him forgive them. He requested St Faustina to have a picture painted depicting him with two brilliant rays of light pouring from his heart, one red and one white. The red represented his blood, and the white represented the water that flowed from his heart. He invited people to stand beneath his cross, so that they might be washed clean in the blood and water. This provides an extraordinary privilege for me, because I get to stand with you there at the foot of the cross; or, to put it another way, you get to stand by my side at the foot of the cross, and you reap all the reward that flows from that supreme sacrifice of Jesus. Besides the extraordinary graces being poured out on you, I think of Jesus making up to me for the lack of support I experienced that first Calvary day. Today is *glorious*, and my heart rejoices. Do you *realise* what is being offered?

Yes, I think I do but, of course, I am anxious to give you my full attention, so that I might understand and appreciate every word that you have to say about it. I don't want to miss anything of this wonderful offer, so I'm depending on you to teach and guide me.

Thank you. This is something I take very seriously. Jesus is actually coming to *you*, and offering you *complete* forgiveness for every sin in your life. It is nothing short of that. In a later session I will speak of purgatory, and how and why so many souls end up there. Here, however, you are being offered a passport and a visa that will get you straight into heaven. Much of your life may be involved with reconciliation of one kind or another. You experience guilt, regret, misgivings, and remorse, and much of this may never be reconciled. And now I'm telling you that Jesus comes to you, fully prepared to wipe the slate clean, and restore you to your baptismal innocence. If Jesus himself had not come with this message, I don't think anybody would have believed it. As it is, it is still not believed by many. Some refuse to believe, others are indifferent, while the vast majority of people know nothing at all about it. There are those who accept it, and believe it 'up to a point'. It is such an extraordinary offer that they fear there just has to be a catch there somewhere! It seems too simple, especially for those who were brought up on religion, which was based on you working hard to save your soul.

Please continue as you are, but I just have to ask this question now, when I think of it, because I might forget it later on. What about my parents, and those that went before them? They really worked hard to 'save' their souls; they prayed, fasted, and were scrupulous in their observance of church rules, practices, and teachings? Now you say that total forgiveness is being offered freely, and the conditions seem to be very minor indeed.

Yes, I understand exactly what you mean. The problem here is one of emphasis. Those who went before you were good people, and they are very close to God, both in affection and in reality. They followed their consciences and the church teachings of their day, and that was the best they could do. Unfortunately, what began as the Divine initiative (God's idea) had been turned into human endeavour (your work) and, even if they still called Jesus 'Saviour', they were really committed to saving their own souls. Of course, they went to Confession regularly, and that was a good thing, but often it was not a Sacrament of Reconciliation, but an exercise of self-condemnation. Reconciliation is a total, complete, and absolute *free gift*, and only God can forgive. Once again, I wish you had stood with me on Calvary, and so much of what I want you to know would have been clearly evident to you. I never asked 'Why, oh why is all this happening?' because I *knew*. His blood was to flow down the sides of that Hill in seven streams that you call sacraments. This was for forgiveness, for healing, for anointing, and for freedom from your human brokenness. You could be made *new* and made *whole* through his precious Blood. The Divine Mercy is not a 'fool's pardon'. It does require certain conditions, although these are very simple. Firstly, of course, it is necessary that you *believe* the reality of the offer being made. It is not some sort of lucky-dip lotto, that may or may not work. When you listen to what Jesus told St Faustina, and she passed it on to you, then you have to be willing to accept and believe that as true, and be willing to act in faith in doing what is required.

The picture of Divine Mercy is important, because Jesus has

gone to great lengths to have it painted and exposed for venera-
tion. He is pointing to his heart, from which are flowing the red
and the white rays of light. He asks that this picture be exposed
and honoured wherever possible. A good start would be to have
this picture enthroned in your house. With the picture you will
receive details of how it is to be enthroned. The next thing is to
familiarise yourself with the Chaplet of Divine Mercy. It consists
of five 'decades', which include repetition of a few short prayers,
which are recited with the help of an ordinary Rosary beads.
You begin with Our Father, Hail Mary, and Creed. Then on the
'Our Father' beads you pray 'Eternal Father, I offer you the Body
and Blood, Soul, and Divinity of Our Lord Jesus Christ, in atonement for our sins, and the sins of the whole world.' On the 'Hail
Mary' beads you pray 'For the sake of his sorrowful passion,
have mercy on us and on the whole world.' You repeat this
prayer ten times, before going on to the next 'decade'. When you
have finished all five 'decades', you pray three times 'Holy God,
Holy Mighty One, Holy Immortal One, have mercy on us, and
on the whole world.' That's it! It's as simple as that! It takes very
little time, but it is a *powerful* prayer. You are standing at the foot
of the cross, offering the sacrifice of Jesus for the whole world.
You are doing what Jesus is doing, except you do not have to
share in the suffering. When you stand at the foot of the cross,
you are at the very *heart* of redemption and salvation. You stand
at the source of grace. Even a pagan Roman soldier struck his
breast in contrition on Calvary.

To continue this contact with Calvary, you are asked to pray
certain prayers at three o'clock each day. These prayers are just
suggested, and they are very simple. You can begin to beg Jesus
to have mercy on all the poor souls who are about to die, and
who are on their way to eternal damnation. No greater act of
mercy can you pray for. 'You expired, Jesus, but the source of
life gushed forth for souls, and an ocean of mercy opened up for
the whole world. O Fount of Life, unfathomable Divine Mercy,
envelop the whole world, and empty yourself out upon us.' The
following prayer is the one most frequently used as the 'three o'

clock prayer'. 'O Blood and Water, which gushed forth from the Heart of Jesus as a fount of mercy for us, I trust in you.'

And that brings us to the Feast of Divine Mercy, which is celebrated on the Sunday after Easter Sunday. It is good that there is no great delay between celebrating the victory of Calvary and Easter, and going on to celebrate the *fruits* of that on the very next Sunday. Jesus has specifically asked that this Sunday should be Divine Mercy Sunday. He asks priests to speak about his mercy on this day. This Sunday provides one of the most extraordinary blessings ever offered by God. If you fulfil the preparation requirements (I will speak of those next) you can return to *your baptismal innocence*, with *all* your sins forgiven. Surely you must agree that that is an extraordinary grace and gift. Had you ever thought this was possible? In our next session, I will share with you about the souls in purgatory. Meeting the requirements of this Novena would have enabled those souls by-pass purgatory, and go straight to heaven. What are the 'requirements'? You are asked to begin the Novena on Good Friday (how appropriate), and recite the Chaplet of Divine Mercy all that week until the Sunday after Easter. It was originally suggested that you go to Confession and Communion *on the day* but, generally speaking, Confession may not be available in most parishes on a Sunday, so going to Confession on the Saturday fulfils the obligation. This was the practice of St Faustina herself. Our whole approach to this Novena should be one of complete trust in the mercy of God, and we should also show mercy to those around us. If we meet these simple requirements, the promises of Jesus will be fulfilled. I honestly believe that this is an offer you cannot refuse. You can, of course, refuse it, but it must surely look foolhardy and irresponsible to do so.

I believe what you're telling me, but I find it difficult to imagine such a generous and extraordinary gift, and it is difficult to understand how anybody could be so blind as to refuse it, or fail to appreciate it. How effective do you see it to be?

It is a source of extraordinary blessings to many of God's people. Thankfully, it is spreading, and more and more people are becoming aware of it. It was given worldwide publicity after the death of Pope John Paul II, who established this Feast. He strongly recommended it, and he put his seal on it by beatifying and canonising St Faustina, the nun to whom this message was first delivered. There are many good and generous people who give of their time and energy in promoting this devotion. This is something that is entrusted to them, just as I am now entrusting it to you. God wants you to announce a *Divine amnesty*, and he invites anyone who wishes, to come to the feast he has prepared for them. Several times, in the gospels, Jesus speaks of the king inviting his people to a feast he had prepared for them. Many of them find excuses for turning down the invitation. One man said that he had bought a farm, and he had to go to inspect it. Jesus must have smiled when he spoke these words, because it's not very likely that a man should buy a farm, and *then* go to inspect it! In other words, what Jesus is saying is that these people do not want to come, and are prepared to tell lies to get out of the invitation. Love is something that needs to be requited. God loves you, but he rejoices when you express your appreciation through loving him in return. You love him when you love others, and the more love you pour out upon your friends, the more love he will pour into your heart. That is why a rejection of this offer of mercy can be so offensive to God. 'What more can I do for my children that I have not done?' As you said in your question, it is amazing that anybody would refuse such an exceptional blessing. However, human beings come in all colours and hues, and they certainly don't follow the same agenda. The same offer is made to *all*. Of course, there are many who know nothing about Jesus, or his mercy. These are people whom the Spirit of God hovers over, and appeals to their hearts for all that is good. *Every person* has a conscience. Have you ever seen a dog that has been doing something wrong? One look, and his master knows he has been 'up to something'. The dog is expecting to be punished, but if his master strokes him and is kind to him, he will go

wild with excitement, and will jump all over the one who forgave him, expressing his delight. There are many others who
know about Jesus but, because of their religious training, they
may not know much about his mercy. For them, God is still a
God of fire and brimstone, and they think as if God did not *really*
come on earth in Jesus, and change things as he did. And then
there are others who know about Jesus, and have *heard* about his
mercy, but they are too busy to bother just now and, anyhow,
they have plenty of time for that later on, when the possibility of
death looms on the horizon. Sad! Sad! Sad! It is very difficult to
do anything with such people. My real problem is that I know
they have the Holy Spirit, just as has every Christian, yet they
refuse to be influenced by the Spirit of Truth who came to lead
them into truth, and to guide their feet into the way of peace.
These are the servants who were given the talents, but who did
not invest them, and had no return to show. 'By their fruits you
will know them.' These people have no fruit to show, despite all
of God's generosity, and the many further blessings and graces
that he offered them. Thankfully, though, there are many who
are responding to the invitation, and the message is spreading to
all corners of the globe. It *has* to be a source of great blessing for
the church, and a very special blessing is that the late Holy
Father (Pope John Paul II) did more than anyone, after St
Faustina herself, to proclaim and encourage this devotion. He
'rescued' it when it was rejected by Rome, after misleading in-
formation had been submitted. He spoke about it on several occasions, and visited the original shrine of Divine Mercy. In pro-
claiming this devotion, he has played a real prophetic role in
today's world. The sins of the world can weigh it down into despair and darkness. There are many Christians in psychiatric
homes, suffering from depression that was caused by their guilt,
which came directly from their religious upbringing. There is
serious need for this Divine Amnesty to be proclaimed. When
South Africa began its present journey, having left colonialism
and apartheid behind, the only way they could 'cleanse' the past
was to set up a Truth and Reconciliation Commission. All peo-

ples involved in the evils of the past were invited to attend this Commission, and tell their story. If they told the truth, they were free from prosecution. If they refused to tell the truth, they were liable to the judicial system. The idea of Confession being part of the requirements for the Novena gives a little hint of this.

There is much literature available on this Divine Mercy devotion, and I recommend that you get your hands on some of it. At the core, of course, are *The Diaries of St Faustina*. You cannot do better than read for yourself all that she was told, all that she saw, and all that was committed to her. I can assure you that you will find it a real goldmine of inspiration. Very seldom do you get such a close-up view of Jesus, his words, his desires, his promises, and his hopes and plans for you. I would go so far as to say that these *Diaries* should be made compulsory reading for all Christians. Of course, I would not make anything compulsory, but I think you know what I mean. I have no doubt that you will find this very inspirational reading, because it contains many direct messages from Jesus, and some from me, and there is an inbuilt blessing in the reading of it. It is so much more than just a book. It is a source of inspiration, and of blessing and, as you read, it will seem as if you were there with St Faustina when the messages were given to her. You may never get an opportunity to visit the shrine in Poland but, even if you did, I would still strongly recommend this book. I cannot honestly see how you could become enthused about these messages, and this devotion, unless you read the book. I consider it as something of great importance. Discovering this precious fount of Divine Mercy puts an obligation on you to become involved in spreading the good news. This part is easy, because, once you have begun to reap the graces, your witness to others will begin. This may involve nothing more than giving a leaflet to a friend, or making St Faustina's *Diary* your special gift to someone at Christmas, or for a birthday. There is a wonderful growth in Divine Mercy Prayer Groups, and quite a lot of countries now have an annual Divine Mercy Conference. All you need is the goodwill, and the Spirit will guide you after that. The gospels begin with a 'Come and see', and they end with a 'Go and tell'. If you come and see, you will certainly want to go and tell. On the other hand, if you haven't come and seen, you will have nothing to tell.

One of the most telling and significant dimensions of the proclamation of Divine Mercy is the timing of it in today's world. It is as if the world is being given one last chance. When the time of mercy is over, it will be followed by a time of Divine justice. Have you ever reflected on the fact that you are alive in today's world? God did not think it a good idea that you should be on this earth two hundred years ago, nor does he think it a good idea that you should be here two hundred years from now. Obviously *now* is the *best* time for you to be living on this planet earth. It is during your lifetime here that this Divine Amnesty is being proclaimed, so it must surely be relevant to you, and to the world in which you live. Life is not a dress rehearsal; you get no second chance at life. This present day will never return, just as it has never before existed. 'Now is the acceptable time; today is the day of salvation.' I can assure you that, despite the havoc that reigns in the world, these are special and blessed times. 'Where sin abounds, there grace abounds still more.' All that is on offer is entirely for your good, and for the salvation of the world. You could not offer God anything more powerful and precious that the Body and Blood, Soul and Divinity of his only Son, Jesus Christ. The sacrifice of salvation is placed at your disposal, and even the words of the prayers are supplied. Nothing could be easier than that. I spoke earlier of those who have never heard of this, and are very unlikely to ever hear about it. What can be said about *you* at this moment? I *know* that you are taking me seriously, and I am truly grateful for that. Of all the topics I could have chosen to speak about today, I chose to speak about the Divine Mercy. I entrust this devotion to you. As you become more and more involved, you will find that it touches each and every dimension of your life. It contains a whole way of spirituality. Your relationship with Jesus will deepen in a very real way, and you will have a sense of 'belonging' in the process of salvation that is being mediated to this world today. I will leave you now, and I thank you for your attention. I feel great joy that I have been enabled to place a most precious and sacred gift into your hands today, and I know that you will treat it with respect and responsibility.

CHAPTER TWELVE

Purgatory

You probably have heard of the Communion of Saints. This is the union that exists between the church triumphant (heaven), the church suffering (purgatory), and the church militant (here on earth). There is a strong connection between all three, and plenty of interaction. Purgatory used to be defined as 'a state or place of punishment where some souls suffer for a while before they go to heaven'. It is much more than that, I can assure you. When a soul leaves the body, it comes into the presence of the All-holy God. Straightaway there is a very obvious contrast. The soul sees itself against the beauty and glory of God, and it can be horrified to realise the vast gap that exists between it and the holiness of God. There are several meetings at the one time. The soul can *now* see clearly what God had created it to become. There is a meeting between the soul as it is, and the soul as God created and intended it to be. The soul is overcome by an enormous sense of unworthiness, and *volunteers* to be purified and cleansed before coming into the fullness of God's presence. It is not a question of God rejecting or banishing the soul, because this precious soul will be with him for all eternity. Rather it is a question of the soul discovering an extraordinary understanding of God's justice, and it would not dare come into the full presence of God in its present state. It voluntarily goes into a state of purification, where it will be washed in the Blood of the Lamb, before entering heaven, wearing the spotless robes of the saints in glory. Time is a very relevant thing in God's view of things, and this time of purification can last for many many years.

What kind of suffering is endured in purgatory? It is as a fire, as I was told many years ago?

It doesn't have literally to be a fire, but it is a furnace of purification. Gold is purified in fire, and all the dross is burned away. The greatest suffering in purgatory is to be separated from God. To have got a glimpse of God, as it were, and to clearly see that, through its own actions, the soul has placed a vast divide between itself and God is a source of great pain and suffering. There is no greater suffering that to be separated from God. Hell consists of every kind of suffering you can imagine. The greatest suffering of hell, of course, is that there is no *hope*. It is the end of the road, and the soul knows that it is there in accordance with its own free will. It will see the endless offers of mercy that were offered by God, and it will see just how much it has ended up in the clutches of Satan, who will hold it up as his trophy of victory. Even in hell, when the world ends, and the battle is over, Satan will still express hatred and vilification towards God. The soul will have become like its master but, without his pride, it may live forever with eternal regrets. On the other hand, the souls in purgatory do live with hope, and they know they will end up in God's kingdom for all eternity. This is some consolation, of course, but it increases the yearning for that reality to come true. The fire is like a strong burning desire to be with God and, while the soul is separated from him, it will continue to suffer greatly. The most difficult thing for the soul is that it cannot help itself. It depends totally on the help of others to shorten its term of punishment. That's where *you* come in, my child. You have an extraordinary and wonderful privilege to contribute enormously to the relief of these suffering souls.

How can I best do that, and could you please give me some guidelines to help me make the most of this great privilege of which you speak?

Your role is a very simple one. The only way you help them is through prayer, and sacrifices you make on their behalf. Just imagine if one of those souls was sent back to earth, knowing what it now knows. How do you think he/she would live, act, and pray? When you do *that* for them, you are helping them greatly. The Eucharist is the greatest source of help for them. As the priest raises the host and chalice, you can ask God to accept this sacrifice for these suffering souls. The Eucharist has infinite power and, if you do as I suggest, there will be many souls in heaven at the end of Mass that were not there when you came in the door of the church. Surely that is not very difficult? Even as I speak to you, there are thousands of Masses being celebrated all over the world. At any moment of any day you can offer these for the souls in purgatory, and your offering will be a source of relief and release for a great number of souls. It saddens me to think that many of my children have little or no regard for these suffering souls, when it is so easy to help them, without making any demands on those who pray. You can place the holy souls at the heart of your daily prayer, and you will constantly become a source of salvation for so many. You can 'people' heaven with souls who are there because of you. What an extraordinary privilege that is! I beg you, please, to take full advantage of the privilege that is yours, so that you will have many voices before the throne of God, who are now interceding for you. It is so simple that you can offer *everything you do* on behalf of these suffering souls. All day long you can be a source of release for them. Do you think that your contribution will not be appreciated and greatly rewarded by them? Of course, they benefit from your offerings, but *you* are the one who benefits most.

The souls in purgatory are a source of many blessings for anyone who contributes to their freedom, and their entry into eternal glory. I said earlier that they cannot help themselves, but they certainly can help you. They can be a source of wonderful blessings for you. This applies even when they are still in purgatory. You can ask them to help you; you can pray *to* them as well as *for* them. You can develop a constant and steady relationship with them, make them part of your life, and be sure and certain that your investment will be repaid a thousand-fold. In them, you have a source of great power and blessing in your own life, while being a minister of healing and forgiveness for them. God has afforded you a unique and special privilege, and you should avail of it in every way you can. During the month of November, the holy souls get special mention. It would be sad, and a great mistake, to confine your interest in them to one month a year. What I am suggesting is something you can do every hour of every day. Before you go to sleep at night, you can offer your sleep as a prayer on their behalf. And again, let me repeat, even as you lie on your bed, you can unite yourself with the many Masses that are being offered around the world at that time, and, indeed, during your hours of sleep. Could anything be easier than that?

You said that the souls in purgatory can help us. How can this happen? Can they be a real source of blessing for us in our own struggles?

Yes, indeed. At the beginning of this session, I mentioned the Communion of Saints. There is a strong bond between all of God's children. Just as the saints in heaven can help you, you can help the souls in purgatory. You will notice that they are called *holy souls*. They are within God's grace, and they will spend their eternity in heaven. They continue to have access to all of God's graces, except they cannot apply those to themselves. In prayer, many people become very preoccupied in praying for themselves. That privilege is not enjoyed by the souls in purgatory. It is as if the purification process is intended to cleanse all self-interest and self-preoccupation, and to concentrate one's attention on the needs of others. You do not have to go to purgatory to begin this, of course(!), but in most cases, this is what it takes to switch the focus of attention away from ourselves to others. Many devout and pious people derive wonderful benefits from the holy souls. They make it an important part of their spirituality, and are abundantly rewarded for it. Concern for the suffering souls generates a spirit of compassion within the human heart and, through this compassion, they share in an attribute of God. The souls in purgatory *can* pray and they *do* pray and, if you choose to be part of their lives, you will be a direct recipient of the benefits of their prayers. I consider this as one of God's special acts of kindness and of love. I know the souls are suffering, but they must get some consolation from the fact that they can continue to do good; indeed, much more good than they could have done on earth. Purgatory, hell, and heaven are *states* rather than *places*. What I mean by that is that the soul doesn't have to *go* anywhere. The suffering souls are very close to you; in fact, they are always in your presence. There are many occasions when a certain soul was allowed reveal his/her presence to a living person. Whether you see them or not, please believe that they are always near you and, indeed, they may often prompt you to pray for them, even if you cannot hear them. They can protect you, and guide you in your decisions. The only way you are going to believe and understand this is by testing it for yourself. Make a point of asking for their help in certain situations, and you will discover that your prayer was answered. As you continue to do this, your conviction about this possibility will become more and more confirmed. You will find many new and good friends this way, friends who will share the glory of heaven with you later on. Imagine the welcome that awaits a soul who has been instrumental in sending thousands of such suffering souls ahead of him/her to heaven. You will be repaid so many times over, that you will realise just how many more souls you could have helped had you made use of all the opportunities presented to you.

Charity in all its forms is love in action. It is correct and right that you should do many kind deeds for those around you. Their gratitude to you, when freely expressed, and the acts that they do to repay you, can serve as an incentive to continue your kindness. With the souls in purgatory, however, you are asked to act in faith, and trust you will see and understand it all at a later time. This is pure and unselfish love, and it is a wonderful tonic for your spirit. Doing a good deed, knowing that it will not be known or acknowledged, is a sign of a genuine loving heart.

With the souls in purgatory, of course, you know that it is known, and is being rewarded just as it happens. However, there will be no clamour or applause, and you will continue your unselfish ministry, without need for public acknowledgement. In fact, ideally, you will come to provide this ministry even if there was no reward whatever for you in it. *Then* it would really be unselfish love. However, God has chosen otherwise, and you should welcome anything that will bring blessings to your own soul. In the everyday Christian community to which you belong, there is a gradual growth of awareness and acquaintance with each other. Meeting people at prayer meetings, or at other parish functions helps to increase your circle of acquaintance, and to make the community become more personal for you. You have many many blessings to gain by becoming familiar with the other members of the Communion of Saints. No doubt you have several favourites among the saints in heaven. It is good that you should cultivate your relationship with as many of God's people as possible, whether on earth, in heaven, or in purgatory. A friend is a gift that you give yourself, and you can have as many friends as you want. I am suggesting that the souls in purgatory can be among your closest and most special friends. You will have wonderful company in heaven when you get there. If you take on ministering to the holy souls as a real part of your Christian apostolate, you will contribute enormously to the glory of God, to the welfare of others and, of course, to your own good. This is something on which you have to make a *decision*; otherwise, it will just be a case of hit and miss. It is not just something you remember when you are at Mass, or when you hear of the death of a person you know. When you are committed to this apostolate, you will automatically include the holy souls in all that you do, and in every prayer you say. It will become part of who and what you are. It will be a responsibility that you will bring with you wherever you are, or whatever you do. It will become as natural to you as your breath. This, indeed, would become a source of constant and real blessings for you.

You may often hear relatives say at a funeral, when speaking about the departed one 'Oh, she went straight to heaven.' Don't be so sure! If you pray for a particular departed soul, who is already in heaven, your prayers will be applied to someone else – perhaps a relative of your own. No prayer is ever wasted. You are familiar with prayers 'for the faithful departed'. That is good, of course, and it should be encouraged and continued. What I speak of here, though, is specifically praying for those souls who are suffering in purgatory, and who need our prayers to assist them on their way. The 'faithful departed' includes, of course, all the souls in purgatory, but I am suggesting that you make a point of specifying that you are praying for the holy souls. I say this for *your* sake, rather for the sake of any group of the departed. By being specific about your ministry to the holy souls, there is less danger that you will forget them, or develop a haphazard approach to them. I insist that your ministry must be constant and consistent. You take on this ministry as a serious responsibility, and not as some whim of fantasy, just because you heard a sermon, or read a book about the holy souls. This apostolate becomes part of your Christian vocation, and you bind yourself to be faithful to it. Of course, if you are not fully convinced of the great importance of this ministry, you will always be lukewarm and sporadic in your contribution. You know that *you* will die and maybe the thought of that might help to motivate you a little stronger! Apart from the great good that flows from your prayers, such prayers are also an investment in your own future. I don't want this to be presented as an exercise in selfishness and self-interest; a 'what's in it for me' job. The fact that you gain many blessings from what you contribute, however, is a just and valid reason for doing a good. Anything that brings a blessing to yourself, or to anyone else, has to be a good.

I will finish now, and I hope and pray that I have set your feet on a very important direction today. I greatly appreciate your help in releasing so many of my children, so that I can hug them, and welcome them home. This is a special ministry that I commit to you, and I know you won't disappoint me. There is so much depending on this ministry. To release *one* soul into the arms of its heavenly Father is an extraordinary privilege that is conferred on you. I will be with you in carrying out that commitment, and when the holy souls pray to me for you, I will smile with delight. Thank you for your attention today, and I ask you to join me now in offering every Mass being offered around the world at this time for the relief of the poor souls in purgatory. Let me stress one simple point just one more time: Our time here has been very precious, and it was good to have time with and for each other. If we both offered the time we have spent as a prayer for the relief of the holy souls, then many of the souls still in purgatory would already be looking at the face of God. I don't mean to infer that, if you take this holy soul ministry seriously, you should/could do nothing else. What I'm saying is that 'whether you eat or sleep, or whatever else you do', you can offer it as a prayer, and many others, including yourself, will be greatly blessed.

CHAPTER THIRTEEN

Heaven

Heaven is the end of the journey, the Promised Land. It is 'over-flowing with milk and honey'. More than anything, heaven is where God is. I know that God is and can be everywhere, but heaven is his home. Once God has gathered all of his children around him, there will be no other place to go. Even if I could explain heaven to you, I would not do so, because it is not possible for the human mind to grasp anything of what heaven is. 'Eye has not seen, nor ear heard, nor has it entered into the heart of a human being to imagine what God has in store for those who love him.' What matters is that God has this in store for *you*! God doesn't really *send* you anywhere when you die. He eternalises the direction you choose to travel in life. The road to heaven is heaven. Once you find that road, it becomes like the pearl of great price which the man in the gospel found. He straightaway went off, sold all that he had, and bought that pearl. You cannot 'drift' into heaven. It is not a question of 'any dream will do'! Jesus calls himself the Way, and he says that no one can enter heaven unless through him. He compares himself to the gate of the sheep-fold, through which every sheep has to pass if they want to belong to the flock.

I know you will speak more about that later on, but the question on my mind at the minute is: What is heaven? *I mean is there* any *way of defining it?*

Yes, there is. During your present lifetime you are forced to live with many tensions, and with all the limitations that go with being human. There is always a tension between what you do, and what you ought to do; how you are, and how you ought to be; what you need, and what you want, and so on. This is part of life, and it is a good, because it is within the tension that all growth takes place. When everything is calm and placid in your life, quite often it is a time of very little growth. The tensions are like the socket in a wall. If there wasn't a negative and a positive, there would be no power there. It is through your own struggles that you develop compassion, empathy, and understanding. When you reach heaven *all* of that will be gone, and you will be all that God created you to be. You will have reached your destination. You will have arrived home to an eternal hug. You will be *free* from all the attacks, lies, and deceits of Satan, and this rejoices my heart greatly. You will be with my other children, and your very presence will render great glory to God, and to Jesus, because your salvation was his present to you. God is not just content with *giving* you something, but he is always particularly pleased when you agree to *accept* something. All of what he does is done with your best interests in sight, and to welcome you into heaven is a very special moment, even for an infinite God whose happiness could not be increased, as you might think. It's unusual, I know, but God does rejoice in your happiness, because it is an extension of his own. Indeed, God thinks of you as an extension of himself, and that is why he wants you with him in heaven. Jesus told his apostles 'I am going away, but I will come back to you, and I will bring you, so that, where I am, you also will be.' Heaven is where you *belong*, and your heart will never be at peace until you arrive at that destination.

When you get to heaven, your heart will be so filled with love and gratitude that you will *need* an eternity in which to express it. Your prayer will be constant, but it will be a prayer of praise and thanks. You will be conscious of all those you left behind, who are still struggling under the burden of their humanity. You will be able to help them, because your *real work* will begin when you reach heaven. There are many thousands of souls on earth who are depending on the prayers of the saints in heaven. Anyone who reaches heaven is a saint, and that is completely independent of whether they are canonised or not. Canonising saints is a way the church uses to teach us what generous Christian living can lead to. The mystics are those whose hearts are so open to God that they can *see* ... they can see beyond the boundaries of human limitations. They are not 'anchored' to this earth, because their thoughts and emotions are preoccupied with things of heaven. Their bodies are still planted on this earth, but their spirits have already gone to share in the joys and glory of heaven. They are constantly aware that they are 'exiles' on this earth, and they have a very real sense of 'home-sickness' for heaven. They long for the day when they will be back home where they belong, because this world holds nothing enduring for them. If they were not 'anchored' in their bodies, they would 'take off', and fly to the very heights of heaven. This longing for heaven is something that is deeply rooted in the human spirit, although most people are not aware of this, and do not recognise it for what it is. Some people go to extreme lengths to satisfy their basic human hungers, and are disappointed when this brings nothing but disillusionment. The gold turns to clay in their hands, and they cannot understand why they are not happy and content with all they have. They do not realise that what they have is something that 'the moth consumes and the rust corrupts'. There is a part of the human heart that is like a part of God himself, and it can *never* be satisfied with things of earth, no matter how attractive, or what satisfaction they offer. Yes, indeed, you were created for heaven, and like a 'homing' pigeon, once you are freed from the 'box' of your body, you will want to fly straight back home. In our last session, I spoke to you about the 'pit-stop'(purgatory) that may await you when you are free of the body. However, you are on your way to heaven, and you know that. That is why you will be eternally grateful to anyone who shortens your delay through their prayers.

Thankfully, for most people, there are many joys along the journey of life, where coming events seem to throw their shadow, and you get just a glimpse of all that will be. This can be very encouraging, and that is why it is provided. You are familiar with the comment of the two men who looked out through their prison bars. One saw the dirt on the road, and the other saw the beauty of the stars. A Christian is someone who lives with eternal hope. They can lift their eyes above the chaos that surrounds them, and they *know* that they 'have not here a lasting city, but look for one that is to come'. It is this hope that sustains them, as if heaven itself came to meet them along the way. People flying to a holiday in the sun can enjoy the flight because of where it will lead them. They didn't spend all that money just to be flying above the clouds, strapped to a small seat, with limited space, and limited freedom. It is the same with people returning home after being absent for some time. They long to see familiar faces, and familiar places. One of the special joys of heaven will be to meet up with many old friends and relatives, and not have to say 'goodbye' again. You will join with those friends and relatives in interceding for friends and relatives who are still struggling along, hoping to join you one day. You will see the grief of those you left behind, and you *know* that 'every tear will be wiped away, and every broken heart will be made whole'. You will have many opportunities to help those you left behind, whether they are aware of your help or not. Once you get to heaven, *everything* else becomes relative. You see the tears of those you loved, and yet, given a choice, you would not dream of returning to them. Like you, they will just have to wait until their time comes to be released from the body, and to fly to the heights. It is said that 'friends are quiet angels who lift us to our feet, when our wings have trouble remembering how to fly'. You can be a wonderful friend to so many, and you can *now* do for your loved ones all the many things that were impossible while you lived among them. I spoke in the last session about the Communion of Saints. This is it in practice, when the cord binding you to family and friends is not broken but strengthened, and much interaction can continue between you and them.

When you get to heaven, one of the things that will amaze you is to see and realise it was all *so simple*. The gospel is a simple message for very complicated people. God is infinitely simple, and that is why it is not possible to 'define' him, or to 'contain' him in words. The message of the gospels is, of course, very simple but, as Jesus said, only those with the heart of a child will understand it. The 'head' keeps getting in the way, in our attempts to understand. The truth is that we will never understand, in so far as knowledge is concerned. The child knows how to switch on a computer or a television set, without needing to know how it works, and why it works the way it does.

Are there 'layers' of saints in heaven? What I mean is, are there saints who have a higher place than others, with those at the top being far removed from those who 'barely made it'?

Heaven is heaven, and once you get there your happiness is complete. Some saints will have a higher place than others, but this will cause no trouble at all. Let me explain it to you this way. If you got an egg-cup, a cup, a jug, and a bucket, and you fill each of them to the brim with water. The amount of water is different in each case, but the reality is that each is as full as it can possibly be. If these were animate objects, each would be content with its share, because each could not possibly hold any more. It is the same with the saints in heaven. Some will have a greater capacity for love than others, just as was the case when they were on this earth. They will rejoice in each other's 'completeness', and they will marvel at the infinite justice and 'fairness' of God. Because God is infinitely great, each soul will feel itself close to him, and each one will be totally happy and grateful for such an extraordinary privilege. They will be deeply aware that, even with all the good they did down here, the whole thing is *gift*, and they are deeply conscious that, no matter how much they did during their earthly life, they could *never* merit or deserve to enjoy the delights that they now experience. For the *first* time in their lives they will know what *real* humility is. They are in glory, they are filled with joy, but they are also very conscious that, of themselves, they *never* could have 'made it' here.

What's the story about the body? I understand that we will have 'new' bodies, as if the bodies we now have could not last for all eternity. If this is so, when does this happen?

Yes, indeed, you are not far from the truth. The body you now have is *mortal*, which means that it will die. When it dies, it will return to dust, and will remain dead. The bestowal of a 'new' body is something that will happen at the end of time, when all of God's children will have arrived *home*. There will be no age significance in heaven. It would be strange if the age span went from 100+ right down to the embryonic age of three months! No, there will be no age difference, and each body will be like a piece of a mirror that reflects some aspect of the glory of God. The shape, size or features will be totally insignificant, because the body will be as if it were transparent and translucent, so that the brightness of the soul can shine through. Light, as you know it, is real darkness, compared to the sheer brilliance of the light in heaven. Each one will see some aspect of God reflected in the others, and God will be the complete focus of their attention. Relatives will *know* each other, just as I now know Jesus, Joseph, Elizabeth, etc. However, the boundaries of family, as you know it now, will be gone, and you will be conscious of being a full member of this beautiful family of God. Just as St Paul said that he was now looking at things 'as through a dark glass, but then I will see clearly …'. The new body you will receive will be one that will be 'fit' for heaven, and it will be free of all appetites and bodily passions. It will be pure as God, and he will rejoice greatly in the beauty of his creation. His plan for you will be complete, and he will rejoice in his creation.

This world is not your home. 'We have not here a lasting city, but we look for one that is to come.' Then you will be revealed in all your glory, and all your hopes and expectations will be fulfilled. There is no way you could possibly understand now what you will be like then, and one of the special blessings is that your joy will not be limited by time, or by capacity to enjoy. Let heaven fill your thoughts, and you will find great encouragement in your present journey. You *know* where you are going, and you know the *Way*, which is Jesus. I will accompany you every step of the way. Death has lost its sting because of the victory of Jesus on Calvary, and on Easter morn. You will see death as a release, not as a punishment, or something to fear. All of that has been removed from the life of a believing Christian. 'Everybody wants to go to heaven, but nobody wants to die!' Death, for the Christian, is as birth was for the baby. It is a passage to something greater. The unborn baby cannot imagine what the next stage of life will be like. Birth is something that 'happens' to it, without any effort on its part. It is the same with death. No matter how many friends stand around your bed, death is a journey that you have to take alone. Nobody can do your dying for you. That is why it is wrong to have what is called today 'assisted death'. That is an abomination in the eyes of God. Death is something truly personal, and is as much part of life as birth is. When a baby is born, the only certainty that can be predicted is that this baby will die one day. Death is certain; it is life that can be quite uncertain at times. The Christian should be able to embrace and welcome death, and see it as a release from the prison of the body, allowing the soul to soar to heights beyond your wildest dreams. It is important that the Christian comes to terms with death, and accepts it as a fact of life. It is not the *end*, but the *beginning*. When the soul leaves the body, it can now become everything that God created it to be. Its exile is over, and it is free to go home. You will no longer need the body, which can be disposed of as you or your family decide. Some bodies are buried in the clay. Others are cremated, while others are donated to science to advance medical research. Many dying people donate organs to assist others who may be depending on an organ to survive. This is a generous gesture, even in the face of death. The person who can do this in death is someone who has been generous in giving during life. 'As you live so shall you die.' How you face death is a very good test of the depth of your Christian hope and belief. All that has gone before has been a preparation for this moment. A Christian is someone who does his/her dying during their lifetime. Christian living demands many forms of dying to self. When was the last time you died for someone? If you wait till the end of your life to die, it could be too late. Focus your attention on heaven, and get on with the dying now. This 'dying' is a source of life for others as well as for yourself. It is in dying that you are born to eternal life. You ask me constantly to be with you 'now and at the hour of my death'. This is a prayer that I delight in answering, and you can be assured that I will be there with you, and for you. Just as we are together here today, so we will still be together as you pass on to the third and final stage of life. Enjoy the journey of now, and leave the rest to me. I ask you to trust me on this one, because I would/could never desert you at such a moment.

Thank you for your attention today. Please think about what I told you, and trust me to fulfil every promise I make to you. I am looking forward to having you with me in heaven, and I hope that you, too, are beginning to feel the same. If you can do this, then you are already sharing in the fullness of Jesus' victory, where death is no longer an enemy, but a passage to the fullness of life. I will pray for you now, and at the hour of your death. Thank you for coming to my Playschool, and please feel free to drop in any day for a chat. I am always here, awaiting your visit, your question, or your request. You honour me by involving me in your life. Thank you.